EVER IN THY SIGHT

31 Devotions on the Psalms

EVER IN THY SIGHT

31 Devotions on the Psalms

ABRAHAM KUYPER

Translated by James A. De Jong

LEXHAM PRESS BELLINGHAM, WA
2020

Ever in Thy Sight: 31 Devotions on the Psalms

Copyright 2020 Dutch Reformed Translation Society

Lexham Press, 1313 Commercial St., Bellingham, WA 98225
LexhamPress.com

Print ISBN 9781683593584
Digital ISBN 9781683593591
Library of Congress Control Number 2019951223

Lexham Editorial: Todd Hains, Danielle Thevenaz
Cover Design: Joshua Hunt
Typesetting: Abigail Stocker

CONTENTS

INTRODUCTION

Leaders shape a vision that inspires a following. An inspired following effects change—hopefully, change that is positive and blesses others.

But how does a major leader for good sustain their vision? Clarify it? Expand it? Deepen it? How do they avoid becoming larger than the vision? Preoccupied with self more than with the cause? Compromising their integrity? Disappointing and shattering their following?

The Christian landscape is littered with examples of leaders who began well but went rogue. This, by God's grace, did not happen with Abraham Kuyper. Why not?

You are holding the answer in your hands. He maintained a lifelong, intimate walk with the Lord—a walk reflected in his written meditations, a selection of which are published here.

Abraham Kuyper was born in 1837, the son of a Reformed pastor in the state church of the Netherlands. He distinguished himself as a brilliant student at the University of Leiden who was accorded high praise for his doctoral dissertation. Rejecting prospects for a stellar career as a university professor, he chose the life of a village pastor, confident in his modernist approach to the Bible. Many in his parish were unimpressed by his preaching, but he became increasingly impressed by the depth of their faith and by their exemplary lives. Wisely, he consulted a simple but highly respected Christian woman to learn about this life of faith. They struck up a deep friendship, and she introduced him to powerfully spiritual literature that nurtured her faith. Kuyper listened. Kuyper read. Kuyper reflected. He changed spiritually—you might even say that the pastor was converted by his parishioner. He began reading the Bible not merely with the eyes of scientific inquiry but of trustful dependence on the God revealed there. In short, Kuyper began a life of daily communion and walk with the Lord.[1]

End of story? Hardly!

Through this life of newfound fellowship, Abraham Kuyper developed a sense of how majestic, powerful, and compassionate God is. He came to know God as Father and his Son, Jesus Christ, as his personal Lord and Savior. Kuyper responded in adoration and praise.

---

1. See Michael R. Wagenman, *Engaging the World with Abraham Kuyper*, Lived Theology (Bellingham, WA: Lexham Press, 2019), 11–25.

His reason for living became to serve this God—in everything, completely, with total devotion.

Kuyper cast a vision for what the Christian community could and should become in all of life's endeavors. He began a weekly religious paper to articulate and spread the vision. He resigned his pulpit for a seat in the Dutch parliament. There, he championed the cause of biblically informed justice for Christian schools, labor relations, colonial policy, commercial enterprise, and all things impacted by legislation. He began a Christian university to create space for scientific inquiry shaped by the Christian faith. He wrote and spoke with insight and inspiration on family life, marriage, parenting, church life, worship, and charitable service. He produced substantial theological work that renewed the vision of church leaders. His work—he would undoubtedly have called it his calling and service—created a following that became a movement. The movement succeeded in electing him as the country's prime minister for a term. But Kuyper aged, and the movement gradually fossilized during his later life and afterward. That's the risk run by Christian organizations and structures born of vision. It happens when leaders and followers compromise in walking humbly with their Lord. The vision fades, and human effort and organizational preoccupations become the focus.

What is truly amazing about the life of Abraham Kuyper is that he determinedly maintained his walk with his God until the very end of his life on earth. He achieved this by separating himself once a week, every Sunday, from his daily responsibilities in order to meditate on Scripture and to pray. Out of this weekly encounter with God he wrote a meditation, articulating what he saw and envisioned as he communed with his Maker that day. In writing the meditation, he was walking with God. With rare exceptions, Kuyper kept this weekly appointment with God. Beginning in the early 1870s, he wrote these weekly meditations until the week before he died in November 1920. They were published in his weekly religious paper; in all, Kuyper published more than 2,200 meditations there.

Kuyper's devotions also inspired a following. They were models of daily walking with the Lord. They cast a vision of God and communion with him. They express triumphant faith while categorically rejecting human triumphalism. They appeal to Christians of all social standing, especially those like the woman whom the Spirit used to open the doorway to the Bible for Kuyper. Such people read him gladly, expectantly, every week.

What appears in the collection reprinted here are thirty-one meditations on Psalms. Most were written by Kuyper in his early forties, between 1877 and 1881. They are taken from *Honey from the Rock,* a two-volume assortment of two hundred meditations reprinted in book form in 1880 and 1883, respectively.[2] The title is based on Psalm 81:16: "I will satisfy you with honey from the rock." The meditations are taken from all major sections of the Bible. Interestingly, more are based on Old Testament texts than New Testament ones. The thirty-one psalm meditations are the most from any one biblical book.

The Psalms are important biblical passages for personal devotions and liturgical responses. This is undoubtedly because they are "an anatomy of all parts of the soul," as John Calvin stated.[3] They speak to a wide range of human emotions and conditions, and they do so on an intimately personal level, with unsurpassed depth and insight. They cover the emotional spectrum from lament to ecstatic praise and thanksgiving. The grip of sin and brokenness as well as the deliverance, comfort,

---

2. Abraham Kuyper, *Honey From the Rock: Daily Devotions from Young Kuyper,* trans. James A. De Jong (Bellingham, WA: Lexham Press, 2018).

3. Preface to the Reader, Psalms comm. CTS 8:xxxvi; CO 31:15.

and reassurance we crave appear in the Psalms. Kuyper's meditations reflect all the foregoing and so much more.

Ultimately, Abraham Kuyper's meditations on the Psalms bring people into communion with God. They share his beatific vision of the God of grace for all who truly come to him.

James A. De Jong
Grand Rapids
Trinity Sunday 2019

1 *That man is blessed who does not walk in the counsel of the wicked,*

nor stands in the way of sinners,
    nor sits in the seat of scoffers;
2 but his delight is in the law of the LORD,
    and on his law he meditates day and
    night.
3 He is like a tree
    planted by streams of water
that yields its fruit in its season,
    and its leaf does not wither.
In all that he does, he prospers.
4 The wicked are not so,
    but are like chaff that the wind drives
    away.
5 Therefore the wicked will not stand in the
judgment,
    nor sinners in the congregation of the
    righteous;
6 for the LORD knows the way of the
righteous,
    but the way of the wicked will perish.

1

DEFINITELY BLESSED

Isn't it wonderfully profound that our Psalm collection dares to begin with a sinful, lost, no-account man who is struggling in misery, dying in his distress, and mouthing one complaint after the other, but who is still blessed? No, blissful! Even praised as definitely blessed!

Not only definitely blessed in the hereafter, but already now. Not that that man will be definitely blessed, but that that man is already definitely blessed.

Everyone knows very well that we yearn for happiness in our hearts. All human striving and endeavor is directed to that end. They are attempts to remove the hindrances that impede the way to our happiness. We don't and we can't rest until we are able to say that we are blessed.

"To be a blessing to the poor" is the approach taken, the promise made, and the prophecy announced by every form of idolatry. It's the same with every reformer, crusader, philosopher, and world conqueror. And the afflicted masses turn away from such people after they see that the promised blessedness hasn't arrived. Then the sting of discontent produces even stronger unrest in their hearts.

But now consider your Bible, God's Word. It also makes an approach, offers a promise, and announces a prophecy of blessing to you. But it is much stronger and more powerful in tone than the longing created by the crusader's approach. This Word doesn't only promise less suffering and to ease pain but offers an infusion of real blessedness. And that happiness is so complete that it can even be called "definite blessedness." You can drink that kind of blessedness in such deep drafts that even the term "definite blessedness" is inadequate. That language can't begin to capture the full richness of the peace and joy involved here.

But how and in what way does the Bible promise that kind of definite blessedness?

To understand that, simply open the book of Psalms and notice how in many places the man who doesn't want to walk in the counsels of the wicked is wasting away.

You would think that God would deliver him from all his illnesses. But notice how he complains in his chains, calls out from the deadly dangers he faces, and simply moans in the bottom of some pit where there is no water.

You would think that his cup is brimming over with prosperity and wealth, but instead you see that he is hunted down like a doe in the mountains and that all the waves and breakers of the Almighty are crashing over him.

You would expect that he would be surrounded by a circle of faithful companions. But notice that all his acquaintances have abandoned him, and that the man who ate his bread has repaid him with affliction.

If then all these earthly blessings continue to be threatened, you would at least imagine that this most blessed of men would walk in quiet peace before the face of the Lord and enjoy uninterrupted holiness and devotion. But you find just the opposite, for over and over again his lips complain about his sin, and he prays for forgiveness. What rumbles from the bottom of his heart are the struggles that leave him a broken man and a contemptible sinner in his own eyes.

You might ask how it is possible that Scripture still calls such a person "definitely blessed." My good reader, here is the key to that wonderful secret.

That man is the most miserable of all people in every other respect. No one has said it better than Paul did: "O miserable man that I am. Who shall deliver me?" But in one respect the page is completely turned, and that's precisely where salvation emerges. That man knows that it's not he who possesses God, but God possesses him! He lives by and with that faith. That's all he needs. He doesn't desire more. Now the pit without water becomes God's pit. God put him there. God is working in him there. God wants to lift him out of it, and he will.

So do you understand now?

Definitely blessed because God possesses him, God upholds him, and God wraps his soul in the bonds of his divine will. Those bonds tie him securely to Christ, the Son of his love. God is present in his Son and present in himself.

This is truly a miracle. All those other proposals, plans, and strategies for making people happy have long ago been discarded, mocked, and then forgotten, and the multitudes in their inflamed bitterness have stopped following those who made them false promises. Then the plan in the book of Psalms for finding definite blessedness emerges once more. It's three thousand years old now. But in every land and among every people you still find living examples of which the Holy Spirit describes: "Look over there! There's the kind of definitely blessed person I'm talking about!" And if you were to take the entire world together, there would be a whole multitude that would be celebrating and saying in unison: "Yes, I'm one of those who have experienced that glorious grace!" You'd be able to hear over and over again how those people who are hunted and hounded are still singing. Sometimes they are lying in a deep pit. Sometimes the lions are growling around them. That's when they sing their way through their fears and even rejoice in their pain and oppression: "As far as my situation goes, it's good for me to be near to God."

Is that how it is with your soul, my sister and my brother? Are you being definitely blessed like this?

⁹ Oh, let the evil of the wicked come to an
end,
  and may you establish the righteous—
  you who test the minds and hearts,
  O righteous God!
¹⁰ My shield is with God,
  who saves the upright in heart.

**¹¹ God is a righteous judge,
and a God who feels indignation every
day.**

¹² If a man does not repent, God will whet
his sword;
  he has bent and readied his bow;
¹³ he has prepared for him his deadly
weapons,
  making his arrows fiery shafts.
¹⁴ Behold, the wicked man conceives evil
  and is pregnant with mischief
  and gives birth to lies.
¹⁵ He makes a pit, digging it out,
  and falls into the hole that he has made.

A GOD WHO SHOWS HIS WRATH EVERY DAY

You believe in the love of God, don't you? At least you confess that the Lord is "merciful and gracious, slow to anger and filled with loving-kindness." A deeper, more unfathomable pity than the tender compassion of your heavenly Father is unthinkable. And it's well that you, who are capable of only stammering your praise, stand amazed at such love and worship him for his compassionate pity.

But, dearly beloved, why are your hearts troubled when the church of Jesus Christ whispers to you—yes, even drums it into your conscience—that this sensitive God becomes angry and even shows his anger daily? When you hear that, why do you turn away, plug your ears, and even beg us to keep quiet about it?

Are you wrong in doing this?

You are deluding yourself if you think God's wrath diminishes something of his eternal love. Or that it limits to some extent his divine pity! Yes, that it even clashes with his mercy to some extent! But are you seeing this clearly? Is this really the case? Are you right about this?

Suppose that the Lord our God never got angry or didn't show his wrath on a daily basis. Would that in fact still make his tender love for you tender?

You imagine that God's anger is a bad thing and a stain on the robes of his sacred compassion. But aren't you misguided in this? Isn't it just the opposite? Isn't the wrath of God one of the most tender features of his loving-kindness? Isn't it the font and source of many precious realities for you and all his other people? Without God's anger, what would the world around you actually become? Now the wrath of God is burning daily as an almost irresistible force in the hard, callous consciences of the children of the present age. It acts like a cauterizing iron on their hearts that sears and shrivels for a time all the boils and abscesses and pustules that are ready to burst and spread their unhealthy filth who knows how far. God's anger working in the consciences of worldly people is like a bit in the muzzle of wickedness. It restrains evil so that it doesn't destroy you, sweep you along in its wake, and poison and corrupt the air around you too much.

God's anger shown every day is the mighty force at work in your own home. It keeps the unconverted members of your household in check. It restrains them by putting a divine foot on the lids of their hearts. This suppresses the ungodliness that would otherwise come to the surface.

God's anger is the guardian of your loved ones when you leave them at home alone or send them off a little way into the world. It protects them when you can't watch over them so closely, set boundaries for them, or discipline them any longer. That's when God's anger does this for you. It takes over where you left off. It is a blessing in the lives of your children who would otherwise be lost.

Moreover, even when you're present with your children, other members of your household, or your friends and when you earnestly admonish them to put an end to some evil or wicked activity, God's anger is at work. You yourself can't do anything about it, and your words are ineffective, unless at the same time God's wrath makes an impact on their hearts and disturbs them spiritually.

To take this a little deeper, suppose that on some occasion or other you became intensely angry over the wicked behavior of your dearest children. You had the satisfying experience of venting your anger in a tender, holy, earnest, and passionate way. Then weren't you able to thank God that he let you share his anger and use you as his instrument? His anger was expressed in yours and gave it a flaming, penetrating power!

But I ask you to think about yourself for a minute. Aren't you indebted to God's anger yourself? Should you overlook what you've been benefiting from for your entire life and what's been yours because of God's anger? Simply allow me to lay out that matter a little further for you.

As you look back on it and remember, you really consider it quite a blessing, don't you, that the part of your life that preceded your conversion was not all that terribly tarnished. You weren't all that humiliated or stained by your sinfulness. You understand perfectly well that you're not a hair's breadth better than someone else who's fallen deeply. You recognize that nevertheless you deserved to be lost for eternity. But looking back, you realize that for you it's been relatively less agonizing or grievous. That's because you were dealt with charitably. That in itself is a gift! So how do you explain that charity now? Was it a gift granted because you were so careful about not being corrupted or humiliated? Admit it, my brothers and sisters. Wasn't it because the wrath of God had made such a sharp impression on your soul and the souls of your caretakers? It was so unrelenting in its opposition to ungodliness that even though you wanted to take a swim in the river of unrighteousness, you didn't dare to jump in. In fact, you really couldn't!

That's the first point I ask you to think about. Here's the second.

During your conversion, wasn't God's anger at work just as strategically as his sacred mercy? Both were instruments he used. In fact, if the Lord had not used his anger in this connection, would you ever have been converted?

I know very well that there are many people who think that it was only the enticing sound of the King's invitation that attracted them, like the soft and cool evening breezes after a hot day. But isn't that a delusion and self-deception? Wasn't the soft, cool breeze preceded by an earthquake and the earthquake by a powerful wind? Would that enticing invitation ever have attracted you if it had not been preceded by restlessness, some disturbance, or a convulsion in your soul? Would you ever have broken with the world if God had not first raged against the world in your own heart? Didn't you feel something for God's law at the time? And does that law ever work without anger? Would you ever have known what divine compassion is, to briefly summarize, if your terrible carelessness had not first been hounded by a sense of God's wrath?

And now the third point.

The big event has now occurred in your life! Everlasting praise and honor be given to God for this! The Spirit testifies with your spirit that there is now an "Abba, Father" to whom you can appeal. And for the rest of your life your resounding song can be: "I was lost. I was lost. I was lost, but now I've been purchased by my Lord!"

But now it might be asked of your soul how you're going to conduct yourself in that new status. Are you finished with the world, or are you still in it? Have you gotten rid of your sin, or do you still struggle with it? Is the battle won, or do you wage it every day? Have you grasped this, or do you still strive to do so?

And what does the experience of God's most precious children teach you in this regard?

It teaches that from the very first days after their conversion they've been kept busy with unmasking Satan. It teaches that from the beginning Satan's henchmen have been deliberately aiming their poisoned arrows at their hearts. It teaches that the world, like an adulterous woman, has been working from the outset to tempt their souls. You can safely add that God's children have learned that from the time Christ first laid his hands on them they've known that they still carry around an ungodly heart in their chests. They know that their souls are graves filled with dry bones. Be sure of this: when an unconverted person is exposed to Satan's temptations for as much as one moment, they cave in and their fall is tremendous. It's not the same for a child of God, who comes through it triumphantly.

If this is how it is, therefore, let me simply ask this. Who is your helper in all this frightening conflict? What power is available to help a child of God get through it triumphantly? Just admit it! Isn't it God's anger?

This is the anger of God that allows you no rest. It's an anger that visits half-hearted efforts with lashes of reproach and self-criticism. It's a holy indignation that afflicts you so deep in your loins that you crumple with pain. And when Satan numbs you half asleep, it's an anger that pierces your heart so intensely that you're shocked awake. Your head snaps back, and wide-eyed, you immediately see that you've reached the point of offending your God with your terrible wickedness.

Do you really want to wish away that kind of anger from God? Do you really prefer love without such anger?

Wipe such unholy language off your lips, brothers and sisters. It's much better that you pray with all God's people: "O Lord, my Lord and my God, please let your anger continue to bless me. Show me your anger every day, every day that I still feel afflicted by sin."

1 *My God, my God, why have you
forsaken me?
Why are you so far from saving me, from
hearing my groaning?*

2 *O my God, I cry by day, but you do not
answer,
    and by night, but I find no rest.*

3 *Yet you are holy,
    enthroned on the praises of Israel.*

4 *In you our fathers trusted;
    they trusted, and you delivered them.*

5 *To you they cried and were rescued;
    in you they trusted and were not put
    to shame.*

6 *But I am a worm and not a man,
    scorned by mankind and despised by
    the people.*

7 *All who see me mock me;
    they make mouths at me; they wag
    their heads;*

8 *"He trusts in the LORD; let him deliver
him;
    let him rescue him, for he delights in
    him!"*

3

ELI, ELI, LAMMA SABACHTHANI!

To say that our Lord and Savior, when dying on the cross in his dreadful fear and anguish, was thinking about Psalm 22 is basically to undercut Scripture. To think that he was consciously quoting its opening words when he cried "*Eli, Eli, lama sabachthani*," is to diminish the person of our Mediator.

Or to come at it from the opposite direction, to suppose that God in his omniscience, because he already knew ahead of time what Jesus would say on the cross, had David write what he did, would be to impose external human standards on God! It would reduce the work of the Holy Spirit to a polished mechanical composition.

No, to retain Scripture as the divine work of the Holy Spirit, Christ as the eternal and faithful witness, and God as true God, all such artificial and superficial guesswork has to be swept aside. These words have to be understood in all of their exalted, godly character.

Christ understood the nature of his suffering from the outset. Not because someone explained this to him, but because of the nature of suffering itself! Death is not something capricious, but its terrible perverseness is determined with exact precision by contrast with the very essence of life. What can also be determined are various levels of suffering in death. You can talk about experiencing it more deeply, less deeply, very deeply, or even sinking to the very bottom of its depths! What can be ascertained with great exactness and precision is how people experience death in proportion to the tenderness of their individual emotions, the strength of their respective awareness of life, and the degree of their own holiness. This is all determined not by some precise external measurement, but by the very nature of life, the character of destruction, the hellish depth of death's perversity, and the complete sensitivity and holiness of Jesus' totally sinless humanity.

Christ did not have to guess what was coming! He knew! He knew in the most exact and unique way possible. There was no uncertainty involved here whatsoever.

This is the Christ who was the inspiration of his church ever since the days of Paradise. This is the Christ who felt oppressed in all the oppressiveness that his people experienced. This is the Christ who from of old comforted his faithful as "the face of an angel."

This is the Christ, says the apostle Peter, who governed prophecy. In prophecy and through the Holy Spirit, he revealed himself, announced his own life, and predicted his own future. He even disclosed himself in the shadows so that the church of the old covenant could already be enlivened by the everlasting beauty of the Mediator and be justified by faith.

The Scriptures of the old covenant didn't merely announce him. He himself is the substance and content of the old covenant's Scriptures. He animated them. He brought them. He gave them to his church as a gift of his grace.

He gave her these Scriptures not as an external jewel, but as the avenue by which he came to her. He revealed himself to her in these Scriptures before he came to her in person, sending her images of his likeness, if we may put it that way. Abraham and Moses, David and Solomon, Job and Isaiah, and whoever else you might name are instruments whom he created to convey features of his likeness. It prepared the way for recognizing him when he came. And now, in retrospect, they describe for us all the fine points and tender features of his full work as our Mediator.

When the words *"Eli, Eli, lama sabachthani"* crossed David's lips, they amounted to the anticipated experience of Christ's frightful pain in his soul that was coming on Golgotha. This occurred by virtue of the definite qualities of human nature and their assured response to the depths of death that would inevitably come to expression then. What a terrible event that would be when the dreadfully frightening lament of "*Eli sabachthani*" would arise from Jesus' constricted throat as he made his last gasps.

Just as today we are sometimes given the privilege of bearing the scars of our Lord's suffering after Golgotha, so also a few of the elect under the old covenant were accorded the privilege of bearing the scars of the Lord's suffering before Golgotha. The Man of Sorrows is depicted beforehand in Jehovah's Suffering Servant. The entire body of believers already then was asked to bear to some extent a faint reflection of those scars of the cross. But only one man of God was assigned the honor of being set aside to bear them fully. That man was David.

Two things are noteworthy in the case of David. The first is that he had definitely been thrown into "the deepest pit that held no water." The second is that when he poured out his frightened lament about his own suffering, the Holy Spirit chose him as the instrument for revealing the Messiah's suffering. The tone of his complaining was immeasurably deepened when by inspiration his lips expressed total abandonment. The full reality of that abandonment then had to be conveyed by the lips of Jesus directly, not now through the work of inspiration.

This is how the experience of Golgotha lived ahead of time came to be expressed in the lament found in Psalm 22. The cry of hellish anguish arising from Christ's soul on Golgotha neither merely echoed it nor added anything to it. It was torn from his weakening soul at that moment and of necessity had to cross his lips. It conveyed how frightful his death was and the immeasurable depth of his emotions.

He, the eternal Word and the Son of God, was also human. He was flesh and blood. He was like us in every way, sin excepted. In the most intimate and tender way imaginable, he had united our human nature with his divine nature. Nothing whatever of his Godhead was diminished. How could it have been? And yet in his tender mercy, he arranged it that the human nature remained completely intact, which is completely unexplainable for us. This would make it possible for us to testify: "Yes, he truly does bear our flesh. He became one of us!"

And once he did, he entered into what is ours. Into our deep sorrows! Into our sinful and perverse lives! Into the shambles that make up our world! Into the catastrophe that we call human life! Walking on the appalling, subversive, and turbulent terrain beneath which hell's volcano lies concealed! From that hell, the thick smoke of death filled with the wrath of God rises. Heavy as lead, it settles across all of human life, which is cursed and doomed to destruction.

While everyone else avoided that and attempted to hide from it, he had to enter into it. While by God's marvelous grace they still had protections from it and could temporarily avoid its terrible, deadly destruction, the same was not true for him. He had to willingly go out looking for it. He had to concentrate on it completely. He couldn't rest until he had tasted the deepest and most bitter aspects of that death.

We're not talking here about death as we view it. We're talking about the death that lies even beneath that, death that culminates with falling into that deep, eternal pit with its hellish oppressiveness. That's where the wrath of God against all that is not holy clings to death.

We're talking about that death that is completely contrary to living. And God is Life. Death, therefore, is God's enemy. God pushes back against it. Sin is death. All sin is death. Because God is Life, he can do nothing else but pour out his everlasting anger against sin and death.

Even although you can never resolve or explain this matter, this much is sure. Either your Savior has tasted death or he has not. If he has not, where then is your hope, O you children of the kingdom? If he in fact has, then please tell me, you who call yourself one of the redeemed, which death has your Savior suffered for you? Merely the death of entering the grave? Or was it death in its deepest dimensions, with its hellish anguish, and where the wrath of God was fully poured out?

Then woe to you if you are not one of God's redeemed, for then you will have to bear this on your own! But that's impossible, isn't it? For then he's not your Savior!

But he bore it all for you! He experienced this essential death: death in its eternal depth, with all its hellish anguish, in the clutches of God's wrath!

Is it possible to actually experience that kind of death, and not just give the appearance of doing so, without feeling completely cut off from life for even one small moment?

So don't argue about a thing like this and desecrate something so sacred! Just believe it. Adore God for it. Thank him for such unrepeatable and matchless mercy!

This stands fast: the hellish anguish of the depths of death and God-forsakenness is either yours or his to bear.

This is when he said: "I did it for you, O my redeemed follower!"

This is when he was forsaken, and when God's angels heard it from his own lips: "*Lamma sabachthani!*"

For what reason?

So that you would never have to be forsaken by God but someday would dwell with him forever.

And this is by sheer mercy!

⁴ *In you our fathers trusted;*
they trusted, and you delivered them.
⁵ *To you they cried and were rescued;*
in you they trusted and were not put
to shame.

⁶ But I am a worm and not a man,
reproached by others and despised by
the people.

⁷ *All who see me mock me;*
they make mouths at me; they wag
their heads;
⁸ *"He trusts in the Lord; let him deliver*
him;
let him rescue him, for he delights in
him!"
⁹ *Yet you are he who took me from the*
womb;
you made me trust you at my mother's
breasts.
¹⁰ *On you was I cast from my birth,*
and from my mother's womb you have
been my God.

4

A WORM AND NOT A MAN

M an must become a worm and the worm a man!
Doesn't that one profound thought capture the
mystery of our precious, sacred gospel?

Passion Week is unfolding once again, and the church
needs to give a responsible account of Jesus' cross as
though things were happening in front of its very eyes.
But what is preaching on Christ's sufferings except depict-
ing step by step how the Man of Sorrows became a worm
and finally crumpled in the dust of death?

The first mystery, namely that of Bethlehem's crib, por-
trays for you how he who was God became a man. The
second one, in which the cross of Golgotha is the central
feature, shows you how that man was lowered and humiliated in becoming a worm.

"After me is coming One," cried John the Baptist, "who
was before me and whose shoelaces I am not worthy to
stoop down and unloose." In doing so, he was alluding to
the One at Peniel referred to in Genesis 32:24: "A Man
wrestled with Jacob." And to the One in Joshua's vision of
whom it is said: "He looked up and saw a Man standing

25

in front of him" (Josh 5:13). And to "a Man as though clothed in linen" seen by Ezekiel and Daniel! And to the same Man who "stood among the myrtle trees" before Zechariah (Zech 1:10)! And the One of whom it was prophesied that "this Man would be a shelter from the wind" (Isa 32:2)! And "a Man whose name would be 'the Branch' " (Zech 6:12)! And to the One of whom it would be said in that hour of terrible reckoning: "Awake, O sword, against the Man who is my companion" (13:7)! And he was alluding to the One whose deeply felt name for that reason would be "Man of Sorrows" (Isa 53:3)!

Power, strength, and majesty are conveyed in that Man. Together we all flee to him for comfort and protection—the weak, the helpless, and those in distress. And he, the Man of strength, protects us with his powerful arms and drives off our adversaries.

A Man! Yes, that's what he was when he caused the Devil to cower before him in the wilderness. That's what he was when he held thousands spellbound with his words. When he healed the sick and banished diseases! When he cast out devils and they slinked away! When he made the Pharisees shudder by the look in his eye! When he rebuked the storm and calmed the sea! And even more strongly, when he overpowered death and roused Lazarus from the grave! Yes, even in

Gethsemane, when everyone shrunk back from him and his captors fell to the ground.

But could he remain that Man? As that Man, could he break through to what we needed? Could he help you and me by remaining a man? Could he triumph through power? Gain victory by his strength? Could his mighty arms gain the victory?

In response, God's holy Word says "no" and "no" yet again. Unless that Man became a worm, the little worm named Jacob was beyond help. Unless a grain of wheat falls to the earth from above, sinks into the soil, and dies, those who are lost gain nothing. It remains dormant and bears no fruit unto eternal salvation.

Consider this. We really aren't human any longer. All our strength has dried up like a potsherd. Human beings conceived and born in sin actually belong to the dust of the earth. They have become like worms.

Sin has stripped us naked. There is nothing whole left in us any longer. As Comré expressed it so very accurately, even our best deeds give God grief!

One of our glories gives him a little more, the next a little less!

They look good, but in essence they aren't.

We're rotten beams that creak and break under pressure.

We're hollowed out willow trunks in which the night owls build their nests and that are swayed by the wind.

Job fully understood this when he cried: "The stars are not pure in his eyes. How much less a man, who is a maggot and no more than a worm!" (Job 25:6).[1]

Oh, even if we wish this were not true, we see that it is. In God's eyes, we are like those poor little worms that crawl around in the dirt! But this is not what a rotting joist wants to hear! Not at all! It passes itself off as a sound beam and wants to be regarded as the kind of support that can hold up under the pressure of a house resting on it.

This is how a worm dreams in its arrogance. It dreams that it is really a man.

What a dreadful way of looking at yourself!

Then that infinitesimal speck of dust opens its mouth and weighs in against God. In its ungodliness, the mere worm begins murmuring against the Maker of heaven and earth.

This is precisely why Jesus had to be laid so low in the dust of death. For no other reason! What you in your proud heart were unwilling to do for your God, he in his mercy would do for you. In this he is the mighty hero!

---

1. This is said by Bildad, not Job. The quotation is from Job 25:5b–6.

The man of glory in all his strength and power! The Lion of the tribe of Judah! And now this Lion allows his mane to fall to the ground. This Hero throws his quiver of arrows aside. This man bows his head. He crumples in the dust and lets the heavy load of God's anger fall on him. He buckles under it and succumbs to the dust of death. As One despised and rejected, he became like a worm creeping through the dust.

He was despised, and we did not esteem him! We didn't because whose heart ever trembles with holy indignation upon hearing this Man lament: "I am but a worm"?

So don't talk to me about how amazing the cross is. Don't come to me singing about the love of Jesus. All the superficial chatter about a descent into everlasting death is only a heavier crown of thorns that you push deeper into the bleeding brow of the Man of Sorrows. Those who talk this way don't understand. They are superficial. They miss it by a mile!

No, every individual who has not yet learned from the Father to fathom these unbearable sufferings at least to some extent smacks the Suffering Servant in the face all over again. They push that worm even deeper into the ground. They trample on his blood.

Not just several of them, but all of them!

You've done it too, and so have I!

But there is only one who no longer does this. It's the little worm of Jacob. And the little worm of Jacob, who might that be?

That's every man and every woman, every young person and every older one, everyone who has been set free and made serviceable. But previously they were intent on defending themselves and they thought: "This is great! Jesus is a worm, and I'm a real man." "I'm a real woman!" But then the Holy Spirit came. He battered their evil, arrogant hearts. He attacked and broke them until they finally learned to regard themselves as pathetic little worms. Then, lying humbled to the dust of the earth themselves, they yielded to their dear Savior. Then they cried out: "I by the grace of God am but a worm, but he and he only is the true Man."

12 *Many bulls encompass me;*
   strong bulls of Bashan surround me;
13 *they open wide their mouths at me,*
   like a ravening and roaring lion.

14 **I have been poured out like water,**
and all my bones are out of joint.
My heart is like wax
and has melted in my inner parts.

15 *My strength is dried up like a potsherd,*
   and my tongue sticks to my jaws;
   you lay me in the dust of death.
16 *For dogs encompass me;*
   a company of evildoers encircles me;
   they have pierced my hands and feet—
17 *I can count all my bones—*
   they stare and gloat over me;
18 *they divide my garments among them,*
   and for my clothing they cast lots.
19 *But you, O* Lord, *do not be far off!*
   O you my help, come quickly to my
   aid!

5

I AM POURED OUT
LIKE WATER

We know from the Old Testament what the New does not disclose, namely, Jesus' inner feelings as his struggle with death intensified. The evangelists certainly tell us what Jesus cried out on the cross. But they don't say what lay behind what he said. They don't explain what gave rise to those cries of anguish.

They couldn't report that because it wasn't obvious. It wasn't something that could be heard. And they had too much respect for their Lord's suffering to simply make something up!

But they really didn't have to say more than they did, because it had already been recorded.

The Messiah had already powerfully poured out the depths of his soul through the Holy Spirit. What he said came from the marrow of his bones. It was expressed in gripping language that was as deeply disturbing as it could be. He was not like one of us. He hadn't taken this suffering on without knowing what it would be like. He didn't go to the cross only half-knowing what was actually involved.

And when he was crucified, he wasn't even partially dumbfounded by how terrible the suffering turned out to be. No, that would have been unworthy of his divine majesty. As the Son of God, he didn't take on something that he hadn't measured in all its depth beforehand. He had calculated its breadth and actually lived into and suffered every aspect of it ahead of time.

What was involved is captured by the Holy Spirit in the soul-wrenching lament on David's lips that we find in Psalm 22. It rose from the top of Judah's mountains: "My God, my God, why have you forsaken me? Why are you so far from helping me and so unresponsive to my groaning?"

So if you really want to know what Jesus was going through in his inner being and what he was ultimately struggling with on the cross, don't look for it in the Gospels. Go back to Isaiah 53 and Psalm 22. Then explain to me why we don't pay attention to these profound laments in our preaching on Christ's passion.

Well now, one of the features that we capture from this psalm of the cross is Jesus' inner meltdown and his emotional weakening and collapse. The Holy Spirit describes this very vividly in verses 15 and 16. He does so in a number of images and a flood of thoughts that make you realize how powerless our language really is to adequately describe this inner weakening of the Messiah.

While still living, the Lord felt like he was already dead and buried because he laments: "You lay me in the dust of death." Pouring out his soul had been cut off because "his tongue was cleaving to the roof of his mouth." He couldn't even voice his complaints. His tears refused to flow because he felt "as dried up as a potsherd." His heart was unable to resist any longer. He had lost all energy and even the will to live since "his heart was like wax and had melted within him." His body was totally powerless and it felt like he was falling apart because "all his bones were out of joint." In short, it felt to the Savior like his entire existence was caving in and ebbing away because he complained: "I'm being poured out like water!"

Where are those now who say that Jesus died as a martyr?

How do martyrs die?

Always upheld by grace! By power poured into their weakened hearts that gives them heroic courage! By an energized faith that keeps them strong and unwavering internally until their last gasp, despite the fact that externally everything is being destroyed.

But what do you see in the case of Jesus?

Exactly the opposite!

No grace, because he was forsaken by his God! No infused power, because drop by drop all his strength was sucked out of him. He was simply tapped out! No heroism whatsoever, because inside he was completely weakened even before that became evident on the outside!

Internally your Jesus had been broken, not strengthened.

But "broken" is not saying it strongly enough to capture the speed with which that emotional desolateness overcame him or how terrible it was. That's why the Holy Spirit reaches for a more powerful image. He doesn't say "broken," but "poured out." This doesn't convey "poured out" in the sense of oil slowly flowing from a jar, but in the sense of water rapidly gushing down the side of a mountain. "Poured out like water" is a forceful, powerful expression designed to help you grasp what Jesus' emotional weakening was really like.

"Poured out like water" intends to convey how one drop by falling pulls the next one after it. That one, in turn, pulls the next and so on with every drop that follows. Together all the water becomes one irresistible force that races and sloshes down as one mighty flood.

That's how it was for Jesus. It began with the ebbing of his strength. That increased rapidly. It swelled and became more intense until all at once it seemed like he was totally in its grip. Suddenly he was poured out like a great river of water, drained of all strength for living, all spiritual courage, and all energy in his will.

This is an image that conveys indescribable weakness. It's a weakness capable of nothing, nothing at all. Incapable of opening the lips! Incapable of lifting the eyes! Incapable of inspiring the heart to stir the will! It conveys a weakening of the pulse. It's weakness that sucks all desire to pray out of the soul. It's the unspeakable weakness associated with fear and anxiety. It describes being so weak that even the thought of being weak takes too much effort for the completely despondent heart.

This is what the Holy Spirit wants you to see with complete clarity about the Jesus you profess. Crucifixion is not the most bitter of all deaths by far. That's not what this passage is all about. Countless people have suffered crucifixion. But no one except Jesus alone, hanging on his cross, has descended into the depths of hell. No one has ever shouldered the burden of God's wrath against the sins of all human beings. Furthermore, no one else by dying on a cross has ever been crucified in his soul, experiencing the unseen and painful weakness of dying a thousand deaths all at once.

Oh, to be Jesus! To be the Son of God! To possess power like that of the Lion of the tribe of Judah, the roar of his death cry was still frightening! And then out of sheer obedience and in tender mercy to be completely willing to descend into that terribly constricting and oppressive condition of total powerlessness and inner weakness! Can't you feel now, you who are so weak and powerless in yourself, what kind of indescribable torture Jesus your Savior felt in his soul? What a price he paid!

But what if he had not done this? What if he had resisted allowing his heart to melt like wax in his inner parts? What do you think? Could he have ever been your Savior? Or isn't your own weakness really not all that absolute and terrible compared with his? Or isn't it fitting that you have the kind of High Priest who descends so deep that he reaches the place where you are, lifts you in his arms, and carries you on high?

Oh, the wonderful mystery of divine grace!

You thought that you were too powerless yourself! But no, not powerless enough, you have to confess about yourself. You have to become totally powerless! Then Jesus will be with you.

Or, to turn this around, however powerless you may be and however close you may be to sinking into total despair, my brothers and sisters, never toss aside the staff of hope. He who once was the most powerless among all the powerless is now sitting on the right hand of power, at the throne of God.

25 From you comes my praise in the great
congregation;
   my vows I will perform before those
   who fear him.
26 The afflicted shall seat and be satisfied;
   those who seek him shall praise the
   LORD!
   May your hearts live forever!
27 All the ends of the earth shall remember
   and turn to the LORD,
and all the families of the nations
   shall worship before you.
28 For kingship belongs to the LORD,
   and he rules over the nations.

**29 All those that bow to the dust will kneel
in his presence, even those who cannot
keep their souls alive.**

30 Posterity shall serve him;
   it shall be told of the Lord to the
   coming generation;
31 they shall come and proclaim his
righteousness to a people yet unborn,
   that he has done it.

6

THOSE WHO CANNOT KEEP THEIR SOULS ALIVE

W ho clings tightly to the resurrected Lord? The One who rose again and had the ability to walk out of his grave? The One who snatched his life from the jaws of death? Who is there that runs to him for help? Who is the person who never lets go of him again, come what may?[1]

Who do you find at springs of water? It's always those who are thirsty. Who attacks their food heartily? It's those who are hungry. Who looks for shade? Those who are overwhelmed by the heat. And who, I ask you to tell me, are those who should run to Jesus, who rose from the dead, and cling to him? Who should never let go of this Jesus who endured all that he did? The people that the psalmist describes in Psalm 22 are definitely good candidates! They are the ones "who can't keep their souls alive"!

Believe me when I tell you that those who have first tried everything else and tried it everywhere else are the

---

1. This meditation was published during Holy Week 1879.

ones who make his most devoted disciples when they finally come to Jesus!

Being alive is what we're concerned about!

People stake everything on living and on maintaining life. They measure everything in those terms. Everything that draws breath struggles and works hard to keep on living. All our struggles and exertion are aimed at living fuller and richer lives. Heart and head are determined to do just that. And by living, we struggle all the time with what it means to be really living.

When life doesn't go like it should and death in some form intrudes on it, we become disheartened. We become discouraged and tense. Finally, no matter how long we may have struggled and pushed the issue, we get to the point of throwing ourselves to the ground and lying in the dust. This whole process represents what's deeply tragic about life robbed of delightful satisfaction.

This explains why we fight dying.

Fools who think that life consists of what's physical do this very superficially by acquiring material things. But those who are wise understand that the soul is the essence and core of human existence. They profess: "I need to concentrate on my soul. The soul needs to sustain my life." So they naturally focus on the spiritual vitamins and medicines that strengthen the soul.

Oh, the ability, the wonderful ability to change a stone-cold soul depends on finding a way of first bringing it to life and then of sustaining it in that life. It's finding a way to do this without rupturing its connection with our bodily existence more than just temporarily.

Then it's all about a footrace.

One person expects to find it in an exceptionally pious, unnatural, and fastidious spirituality. Another does in being honest, virtuous, and conscientious, while a third person determinedly torments their self with charitable giving, thinking this will work some kind of magic for them. But however much any of them frets and struggles in their attempt to act with integrity, it's all useless in bringing them one step closer to what they're chasing. All three eventually get to that point. The man who is superpious does! The one who is totally honest does! And so does the woman who torments herself! For matters don't turn on a good crease in your clothing, or on a good reputation with others, or on resolute self-control. They turn on living and on the life of the soul! It depends on the kind of living that can deal with anything and that never gives up. But sadly, all those spiritual vitamins don't get you a hair's breadth closer to it. For you are simply too weak to achieve what you want and desire, namely, the one thing that determines everything else. You are totally incapable "of keeping your own soul alive."

You have to get to the point of recognizing that fact. You have to express this in words that are not merely mumbled. They have to be completely frank and come from deep in your soul. Your heart has to be in them! In the presence of God and others you have to say:

"No!" "O my God, no!" "O my brother, no!" "I can't keep my soul alive!"

"I wanted to do it. I tried to do it. I worked at it so hard that my soul sweated!"

"I would have done it by myself. I should have done it by myself. I would have finally succeeded if I had just yearned for it passionately enough, wanted it badly enough, and persisted at it long enough."

" 'My God,' I said in my soul, 'surely in your mercy you will not disregard my intense struggling. Surely you will bless it in the end.' "

"But no. The Lord didn't respond like I hoped he would. He, the Holy One, did just the opposite. He demolished all my efforts. His billows overwhelmed me. His strong winds sucked my lungs empty."

"For now I know that he loved me more dearly than I loved myself. That's why he saw to it that all these efforts came to a dead end. That's why all the paths I took were cut off. They all ended in failure, frustration, and disappointment. In the end, all my vain pride died. My willful determination disappeared to my shame. And the result was that I finally admitted what I had not been willing to acknowledge to the entire world: 'I can't do it! I can't keep my soul alive. I'm powerless, despite what I do or attempt to do. Everything that I attempted only succeeded in deadening my soul further. It sapped my strength. It virtually killed me!' "

And if such a person finally exclaims: "To keep my soul alive—that I simply cannot do," they are already celebrating a true Passover. I tell you that if such a person hears once again about a Jesus who arose, a Jesus who was resurrected from the dead, a Jesus who brought his life through all that he experienced and who thereby demonstrated that he could "keep his own soul alive," I tell you plainly, my good reader, that you certainly don't need to tell such a person anymore: "Just go to Jesus!"

"Just go to Jesus?" That person is there already! They already cling to Jesus. His life is their life!

You know, that's precisely the mystery of true faith. In order to see with your own eyes during your Passover celebration that Jesus lives, you first have to see with your own eyes that in yourself you are dead! Oh, life doesn't lie in the excitement and festivity of a celebration.

The Ruler of Life doesn't appear to any other people than to those who lie in the dust and in the shadow of death!

PSALM 23

1 *The LORD is my Shepherd; I shall not want.*

2 *He makes me lie down in green pastures.*
   He leads me beside still waters.
3 *He restores my soul.*
   He leads me in paths of righteousness
   for his name's sake.
4 *Even though I walk through the valley*
   of the shadow of death,
   I will fear no evil,
   for you are with me;
   your rod and your staff,
   they comfort me.
5 *You prepare a table before me*
   in the presence of my enemies;
   you anoint my head with oil;
   my cup overflows.
6 *Surely goodness and mercy shall follow me*
   all the days of my life,
   and I shall dwell in the house of the LORD forever.

7

I SHALL NOT WANT

"I shall not want!" Whoever believes this has arrived! They have peace. They know contentment. They have turned to the Lord with body and soul, spouse and child, in life and in death. They trust the All-Powerful Being, the Complete Provider, the only Totally Satisfying One, and our most highly exalted and absolutely holy Source of All Good.

Such a person understands, reflects on, and knows this in their heart: "I exist because of the exalted God who has created me. When he did, he already knew that there was a place for me in his world. He determined that I have a calling to fulfill in it. And I believe that he is powerful and determined enough to provide me with everything that I need to fulfill my calling. He does so at precisely the right moment."

Whether that calling is prominent or ordinary makes no difference. Perhaps I have to be careful as a boy when I walk under a ladder on which someone else has climbed high to make a repair or to paint the peak. Perhaps I have to stand for my entire life alongside a busy street with a sign inviting people to turn in and buy what I'm advertising. Perhaps a young woman's job of putting up displays in a store window may not seem very important, but she's indispensable. Never make comparisons! Pay attention to your own work, never that of someone else. And definitely never let yourself think or say: "God certainly could have given me something more important to do"! Because if you do, with that single thought you attack God's absolute sovereignty. And the Lord has no patience for that kind of talk. He knows how things should go. He asks for no one else's advice. And when you complain against God without knowing his intentions, you are attacking him and murmuring against how he arranges things.

This is what's primarily involved in the statement "I shall not want"!

The manager of an enterprise gives every employee as much orientation, material, and other resources as they need to do their own job. In the building trades, for example, a contractor gives the rough carpenter basic instruction, the finish carpenter more advanced preparation, and the sculptor the most precise training. But to the lad who assists them, he gives almost no direction at all. But even he lacks nothing he needs. And if he simply accepts his role, he is happy, whistling his tune while he works, and he feels good about what he's doing. He doesn't need another thing.

Be absolutely sure of this. You will lack nothing for the work the Lord has assigned to you in his circle of servants. But when you step outside that role and want to do something for which God has not called you, then this promise definitely doesn't apply to you. Then you will "want" or lack a great deal. The Lord God provides you with nothing in that case. And you won't be able to buy it and you can't generate it yourself.

But if you accept the position where God has placed you, you will definitely experience that you live without apprehension and a load of concerns. Fear and misgivings under those circumstances definitely indicate a lack of faith. This amounts to a lack of faith that you are in your real calling. They reflect a lack of faith that God the Lord rules over all things. A lack of faith that God is all-knowing and really does know what you need! A lack of faith that God has a purpose for which he has considered and calculated all the details! A lack of faith, in a word, that God is really God! That kind of doubt at work in you is really nothing more than God-forsaken despair in your heart. It's the sin of Paradise. It's Eve's horrible wickedness that is now rekindled in your own heart and renewed in your life.

"I shall not want!" This definitely is not to say that you have here a promise that you will bathe in luxury. My dear brother or sister, it might well be that you have to stand in the fiery furnace like Shadrach did. But it is a promise that even in that kind of oven you "will not want." It is even possible that your life is one long succession of disappointments, of suffering poverty, of bitter pain in your heart. It is possible that God has destined you to demonstrate to Satan that however much poverty, suffering, or humiliation you endure, he knows how to nurture your faith and maintain your joy as his child. The Lord God is mysterious in his ways. He causes some to be blind, others to be deaf, and still others to be emotionally ill. But all of these serve his inscrutable purposes. And the only thing of which people can be sure is that in their suffering or in their rejoicing they will lack nothing in dealing with their situation.

How does a person become a martyr? How can someone in living life submit to fire and sword and still sing psalms? I don't know how! And you don't know how, either, because neither of us has ever been given what was assigned to a martyr. They were given what belongs to their situation, but not to ours.

"I shall not want!" may never be construed as a fortress to which we can flee to avoid suffering. The affirmation should only be taken as a sure promise that we will be able to endure it. I would never say that we can endure it to assure us that we will enjoy a happy old age. No, we are enabled to endure it so that we might enter an eternal day following the dawn of our eternal morning.

"I shall not want!" ultimately means simply this: God will never fail us. In God we have the highest, holiest source of all that's good. So what do we really have to complain about?

This applies to both body and soul.

That's why for your body you will lack nothing that is necessary for your soul. Similarly, you will lack nothing for your soul that is needed by your body. The text does not say: "I will lack nothing needed for my body." It says, "I shall not want!" The focus is on the whole person, on you and me as we are.

If we need oil in our lamps, God provides oil. If the garden is parched, the rains come. If you thirst after the living God, God himself arrives. His messengers climb the highest mountains and shout: "Look, your God is here!"

If you stand too tall, God cuts you down to size. If you sink too deep, the everlasting arms mercifully appear to lift you up.

All of your grappling, all of your soul's contortions must come down to this one thing, that you believe. And what do you believe? Simply this: that you have total access to what already exists in God's storehouse, ready and waiting! And that storehouse is Christ himself. Faith is the movement of the soul by which the Holy Spirit dispenses from Christ's storehouse everything that you need.

Do you need good works? Behold, God "has prepared them for you so that you might walk in them." Receive them and give thanks.

Do you need to be more submissive? God the Holy Spirit will control you like a difficult horse with the bit and bridle, and you will grow compliant and grateful. He will humble your resistant heart with faith in the Word.

Do you need faith itself so that you come crawling on your knees but still can't pray? Do you feel like a thick cloud is hanging between you and God? Then your only deliverance comes not by torturing or tormenting or forcing yourself, because such responses only create more intense sin that pushes you even further away from God. It comes by reading God's Word, where it says:

"The Lord is my Shepherd; I shall not want." It comes with the promise in hand and stammering with a quiet voice and a proper attitude: "Lord, teach me how to pray!" Even being able to pray is a gift given by our Lord God when in his all-sufficient grace he mercifully turns toward us.

May God the Lord grant that from now on you never go to bed without having that prayer answered. I realize that perhaps days will go by before true prayer flows freely from your heart. But what does that indicate?

It always says that whatever you might be experiencing at that moment, the most important thing is not the prayer but what you need to learn in your situation. It involves learning to depend much less on your own mutterings so that after a while you learn what godly prayer really is. Then you will come to realize that even the disappearance of a deep prayer life was a gift from the Good Shepherd, one as necessary as daily bread. Then you will see that it was given without your even knowing it is a gift.

Oh, the Faithful Shepherd, who had much preferred to listen to the voice of your suffering in faith, first carved out in you a riverbed along which your prayers would eventually flow. He did this so that you then might lack nothing that you really needed.

PSALM 24

4 *He who has clean hands and a pure heart,*
  who does not lift up his soul to what is false
  and does not swear deceitfully.
5 *He will receive blessing from the LORD*
  and righteousness from the God of his salvation.
6 *Such is the generation of those who seek him,*
  who seek the face of the God of Jacob.
7 *Lift up your heads, O gates!*
  And be lifted up, O ancient doors,
  that the King of glory may come in.
8 *Who is this King of glory?*
  The LORD, strong and mighty,
  the LORD, mighty in battle!

9 *Lift up your heads, you gates.*
Be lifted up, you everlasting doors,
so that the King of Glory may come in.
10 *Who is he, this King of Glory?*
The LORD Almighty,
he is the King of Glory.

BE LIFTED UP,
YOU EVERLASTING DOORS

David yearned with his whole soul to be permitted to build a temple for the ark of the Lord. But coming to him, the prophet said: "That is not what Jehovah wants. He wants Solomon your son to be the one who builds the temple, not you." And when David was sure about this, he didn't grumble or force the issue. He put the matter behind him, and from that point on he was thoroughly excited that Solomon and not he would accomplish this.

What a glorious day that would be when God's ark would finally be carried into the completed temple! It was as if that day had already dawned for him. He envisioned it all, as though it had already happened right before his eyes. The beautiful metals! The high, stately walls! The procession bearing the ark of God, the seat of his majestic presence! It was as though David, looking down on the ark and the temple, saw much farther. It was as though he were looking into the heart of that other David, the one for whom the fathers of Israel were praying and of whom both the ark and the temple were no more than shadows and symbols.

Next he sees that ark of God processing up the holy mountain in all its glory until the procession stops before the wall of fortified Zion. In the wall are gateways, and in the gates there are doors. And it's possible for the ark to pass through them, to be sure, but they are too low and unimpressive. They are too restrictive for him whose glorious entrance was only being symbolized by the ark's procession. So, filled with the Spirit, David sings a psalm. Listen to what he cries out: "Be raised higher, O you gates. Be bigger, wider, broader, and higher, you entrances. Expand, you everlasting doors. Get regal! Don't hold back! For behold, he is coming to you. The King of Glory, the Prince of the heavenly hosts, my heart's inspiration and my soul's desire, is entering!"

This psalm is referring directly to the narrow gate in the wall of Zion's mountain fortress. Here is Jerusalem. Above her rises the temple. And there are the solid walls with their formidable gates and everlasting doors. This is why David sings his psalm of holy exaltation. The ark of the Lord bearing God's majesty is arriving.

Lift up your heads, O you gates,

> Be lifted up, you everlasting doors,

So that the King of Glory may come in.

Who is the King of Glory?

> The Lord strong and mighty!

The Lord mighty in battle.

Then once again:

Lift up your heads, O you gates,

> Yes, be lifted up, you everlasting doors,

So that the King of Glory may come in.

Who is the King of Glory?

> The Lord of Hosts,

He is the King of Glory!

But all of this wasn't real because Zion itself wasn't the reality. Jerusalem was only a shadow. The temple was a shadow. The ark standing in it was a shadow. Even the walls of Zion separating the temple and the city of Jerusalem were shadows. All of it was a display for instructional purposes. It was a representation of reality and an image of what is true. It all pointed to what is enduring and deals with what is real and eternal.

The wise according to the world don't get this. God's church does. And within that church, all God's dearly loved elect people do. That's exactly the reason that the church of all ages didn't engage in guesswork. It knew certainly, definitely, and solidly what it was singing in this song of David: the ark was a symbol of the actual ascension of Jesus into heaven!

In Jerusalem people were thirsting for the living God. But the Lord was living on Mount Zion, and those walls and everlasting doors couldn't be budged. They were causing a continuing separation. The people saw the temple there and knew that the ark was inside it. They realized that that's precisely where the presence of the Lord was dwelling. But then there were those massive walls, and those narrow gates, and those everlasting doors!

But be lifted up, my soul, and be exalted Jerusalem that languishes. A new day is dawning. Salvation is flowing. The King of Glory is coming. The walls are giving way. The massive gates are being lifted high. The everlasting doors are being raised because the Prince of heaven's powerful army is marching in. And you who have been longing for God's coming are singing and celebrating in victory!

What could those everlasting doors really be?

Everything that shuts Jerusalem off from the ark! Therefore everything that acts as a barrier between languishing hearts of unhappy people and the sacred glory of their God.

A door is anything that prevents you from entering. Because it's bolted and barred, it keeps you out. An everlasting door defies your entrance however much you knock and bang on it. It stays shut, as shut as a wall. It remains so tightly shut that it suggests to you that it will never be opened. It is an everlasting door. It will keep you out eternally.

But now the Messiah arrives. God has mercy on those who are miserable and sends them a Savior. How, then, could those everlasting doors possibly keep him out?

In answering that question, the Spirit prophesies through David: "No, and once again no. The bolts and bars will fall off those everlasting doors!" The doors will be flung open for him. The openings will even be widened and broadened for him. The doors will be lifted up so that the King of Glory may enter in all his glory.

But pay attention! The door is still there! It's the everlasting door of the flesh. You're stuck behind it. It won't admit you. The flesh is oppressive. But Christ breaks through it by coming in the flesh. He comes to you through that everlasting door of the flesh. This brings him close to you. He is one with you. He has become like a brother to you.

But you're still not quite there yet. The Word made flesh is definitely your Messiah. But he is so in a way that, while you are with him and he is with you, you are still languishing and shut out of Zion. You are still barred from glory. The wall and the everlasting door are still obstructions for you.

This is why in the flesh you still have to keep working at making progress in the flesh. You have to climb the mountain. You have to climb from the flatness of this world to the heights of heaven. The glory isn't here, but it's up there. While weak here, the Messiah is mighty there and great in his majesty. That's where he is capable of saving you and blessing you.

This required his ascension! To heaven! To the place where weakness is glorified! Where all the power is! Where power and strength can go to work! So that's where your flesh goes, your Messiah in your flesh, in exactly the same flesh and blood that hung on the shameful wood of Golgotha.

Now, finally, those everlasting doors are completely raised and lifted up. Here, finally, the King of Glory enters in. This is your King, church of God. He possesses all the wealth needed to exalt you, justify you, sanctify you, and redeem you completely.

He enters through the everlasting doors into that expanded tabernacle that is not made with human hands. From there your King causes salvation and blessing to flow freely. From there his strength is expressed, and Satan slinks away because those who were ungodly have now been made righteous.

But this is still not the end of the matter.

One everlasting door still remains. It is the door of your own heart that Satan has bolted shut. It is the door of your own soul that he has slammed closed.

How many thousands of times haven't you banged your head against that everlasting door? This became so oppressive that your fearful heart could hardly stand it any longer. You wanted to escape and you pounded on that door, crying: "Open, open up! Show some mercy! Don't let me choke in desperation!"

But it didn't help. You got no response. The door of your sinful heart seemed like an everlasting door.

That is ... until he came! Right? Until the King of Glory came!

That's when from his throne of glory he sent his messengers. They came with the sledgehammer of his Word and beat on that door. Then you realized that where the Word of the King comes, it comes with power. For then the locks are broken. The bolts are shattered. The doors are lifted, and he enters. The King of Glory comes in. The Lord strong and mighty!

Hallelujah!

5 Lead me in your truth and teach me,
    for you are the God of my salvation;
    for you I wait all the day long.
6 Remember your mercy, O LORD, and
  your steadfast love,
    for they have been from of old.
7 **Do not remember the sins of my youth**
  or my transgressions;
  according to your steadfast love
  remember me,
  for the sake of your goodness, O LORD!
8 Good and upright is the LORD;
    therefore he instructs sinners in the
    way.
9 He leads the humble in what is right,
    and teaches the humble his way.
10 All the paths of the LORD are steadfast
  love and faithfulness,
    for those who keep his covenant and
    his testimonies.
11 For your name's sake, O LORD,
    pardon my guilt, for it is great.

9

THE SINS OF MY YOUTH

We all learned this beautiful verse by singing it from our psalm books as children:

Never again remember the sins
That I have committed in my youth.
Remember me in your kindness
That I may always benefit from your goodness.

But in our youth did we ever think or even suspect how the verse from the Psalms on which this stanza is based would bother our consciences in old age? How it would cast our souls entirely on the grace of God?

Every individual among God's people feels sad and burdened about "the sins of our youth." That's because those sins are simply there. They lurk behind you in your memories. You can't get rid of them. They still haunt you. And what is worst of all is that they get bigger every day.

You ask how that's possible. How can the sins of his youth become larger with every passing day for a person well along in years? Look, the answer is obvious and is really very simple. It's by the holy light of God's Spirit that time and again something from your youth is exposed as sinful. When you did it, you didn't see it as sinful at all. But now you are definitely conscious of the fact that it went against God, that it grieved the Spirit present at your baptism, and that you are accountable for it.

Permit me to add this as well: the further along you get in life, it won't get any better. For, if I could put it this way, suppose that in your past there's a part that is white and another that is completely black. And suppose that these are blotches that lie beside each other. Then you have to reckon with the fact that the black one will expand and the white one will only contract until the question finally occurs to you of whether there was anything wholesome there at all.

The sins of youth are doubly disastrous. They amount to the appearance of an angry abscess in what appears to be sound and healthy tissue, or to the steady dripping of poison into what is still developing. Except that for the entire remainder of something's development it wreaks damage and destruction.

The sins of youth! Oh, how they control the formation of a person's entire character, the whole tone of their life, and the total shape of their future.

They eat so deeply into us because youthful character is doubly soft and impressionable. They put at Satan's disposal the boundless youthful energy and passionate spirit that thrives in the hearts of young people.

Oh, who can ever measure the terrible evil involved in those "sins of our youth," including the "secret sins" buried there? For, and understand this clearly, they are not readily detected. People think better things of you. Your youth itself is like a shield that protects you. It causes anyone admonishing you to focus on better things about you. And that's a license for you to persist without interruption or impediment in doing what's evil.

Still worse is that after you commit them, they continue working for as long as you live. Even when you have been reconciled and saved by God's inexpressible mercy, that old enemy is still lying in wait inside you and evil constantly roils up, "as though from a polluted spring," to use the words of our confession.[1]

Oh, where could we hide if we didn't have a Savior who covered the sins of our youth with the burial shroud of his divine mercy? Think what it would be like if you could never get rid of those persistent memories. How frightening that would be for you.

But also think about how inexpressibly gracious it is on the part of God's Son that he stands between you and

---

1. Kuyper is referencing article 15 of the Belgic Confession here.

your youth. And he says to you: "Forget what is behind you. Stretch out toward what is ahead of you." Already from his cradle, he quietly whispers a word of blessed reconciliation to you!

Oh, if our young smart alecks, our children, and our youngsters would only know what those "sins of our youth" will be for a still-unreconciled heart! How they should flee to God. How they should flee from the world's contamination. How they should find their shelter close to him who said: "Let the little children come to me!" That's where his protective grace is at work even for unconverted youth.

Don't underestimate "the sins of your youth," you children! Pray them away before they happen! Fight against them with your whole heart. This much I know: there is no youth without sin. So why don't you turn, heart and soul, to that which is lovely and of good report?

Church of the living God, help your baptized children come to that point. Parents, you especially should do this! So much can be avoided. So much can be resisted. The pores of a child's soul are so receptive. You penetrate them so easily and so undetected through your own sinful surroundings. But the Lord also wants to use you in unnoticed ways to inoculate your children with good medicine.

Once again, "the sins of our youth" represent such a sad and deeply depressing chapter in the history of human sin. At the same time, so much can be done from the Word of God for, with, and in our young people to restrain and limit them as well as remove incentives to commit them.

So guard yourselves, my readers both young and old. Stay faithful!

10 All the paths of the LORD are steadfast
love and faithfulness,
    for those who keep his covenant and
    his testimonies.
11 For your name's sake, O LORD,
    pardon my guilt, for it is great.
12 **Who is the man who fears the LORD?**
He will instruct him in the way he
should choose.
13 His soul shall abide in well-being,
    and his offspring shall inherit the
    land.
14 The friendship of the LORD is for those
who fear him,
    and he makes known to them his
    covenant.
15 My eyes are ever toward the LORD,
    for he will pluck my feet out of the net.
16 Turn to me and be gracious to me,
    for I am lonely and afflicted.
17 The troubles of my heart are enlarged;
    bring me out of my distresses.

10

WHO IS THE MAN WHO FEARS THE LORD?

In our day people in more refined circles speak with a degree of fondness about "seriousness," "living seriously," "being serious," and "thinking seriously." People in both orthodox and modernistic circles do this. In orthodox circles, this means that someone has reached a point of being reflective about their situation. In a modernistic context, it means that a person is not a carouser, doesn't live a debauched lifestyle, and is not enslaved to sensuality but sets their sights on higher things.

In the vocabulary of our century, the word "serious" has gotten wide usage because of its many-sided meanings. It's a word that people use readily and with appreciation. It awakens better aspirations in our heart. Everyone tolerates its usage. It's not entirely misunderstood even in rather superficial circles where now and then it's employed to refer to the serious side of life. It's comparable to the younger children in our aristocratic families, where everyone thinks of them lovingly, like little Benjamins. Thus the tone struck in our era by the image of being serious is such that almost all speakers appeal to it. They think that by talking about being serious they evoke a feeling of warmth and kindle a fire in their listeners. And it's true that the thought of being serious inspires you to do better and is uplifting.

"Serious or fun loving" tells you enough about what being serious involves. People are serious when they no longer joke around about everything. Getting serious starts when all the vain, empty talk stops. The person is serious who hesitates going along with all the lighthearted frivolity of our age that mocks everything that is dear or painful. "Being serious" is the opposite of "being playful" and is in stark contrast with literally making a game of everything from early morning until late at night. Those who are serious mean what they say. They embrace life in its reality. They restrain empty-headedness. Life becomes meaningful for them.

This is all quite wonderful! But it's also a serious indictment on the miserable, dissipated spirit of our age. A person for whom things are meaningful is an exception. So is one for whom life is much more than a game. Let's be clear. You're an exception when you get sick to your stomach of all the empty jabber and unrestrained chatter of the children of our time. They simply laugh and snicker their lives away!

Theirs is the true French spirit whose revolutionary atmosphere has settled over a pathetic Christianity. The French Revolution with its intoxicating brew has made baptized people so woozy that they are ashamed to identify what's good as good any longer. And when they have some need, they blush beet red if anyone catches them in a brief prayer.

These are bad times. Many families, both parents and youngsters—take whichever you choose—are just as entertaining and just as offensive to watch as a cage full of playful, howling, grimacing chimpanzees at the zoo. How often don't you encounter devilish dishonesty? Hellish pleasure in the mocking, devilish delight with what is evil, brutish, or vicious?

In such circles, you are certain to find a serious person, even a devout one, who will speak "a serious word" that falls like a drop of dew on some worn-out soul. Their voice is a call to seriousness. It's an expression of courage, love, and higher purpose. We wholeheartedly celebrate their kind of seriousness. We're pleased when a break occurs in unbelieving circles with what's empty, stifling, and vain. We're enthusiastic when oppression of all that's holy is somewhat diminished.

But should we as Christians then adopt the way the unbelieving world thinks about seriousness, with its emphases? Just because seriousness has somewhat higher standing in these circles with such low standards, does it measure up to the much higher, more glorious ideals set for us by the cross of Jesus Christ?

Understand that the Word of God knows virtually nothing about that kind of "seriousness" and "living seriously." The expressions "with seriousness," "seriously," and "serious" do appear a few times in Scripture. But they do so with a completely different meaning from the way people presently talk about "being serious." "Give serious attention to" in Exodus 15:26 and other places says no more than "listen carefully" to something. To do something "seriously" in Jeremiah 22:4 means no more than "to tackle something with enthusiasm." But you never read in God's Word about a "seriousness" that stands independently, like a distinct virtue that is the mother of all other virtues.

Taken in that sense, "serious" first appeared among the followers of Cocceius.[?] The larger portion of them called themselves "serious Cocceians" to distinguish themselves from the lighthearted impieties of others in their circle. Since then usage of the term has increased

---

1. Johannes Cocceius (1603–1669) was a Reformed theologian who taught at the University of Utrecht, where he became a leading advocate of federal or covenant theology.

to the extent that emphasis on the seriousness of life has decreased. The more that everything was seen as a game, the more obvious it became that people often had to make clear that they weren't "simply playing around." The word that came in handy in making that point was the word "serious."

Simply for that reason the enthusiasm for parrying with "being serious" has become less applicable in a Christian setting. That's just the nature of the situation. There the canvas on which the more ideal images should be alluringly displayed is already beginning to be tinted with this notion of "being serious."

If Scripture wants to get our attention and shake us out of our complacency, and where it wants us to reflect on eternity, it doesn't approach us with the weak directive "Be a little serious now!" It takes a completely different and incomparably deeper approach. It says: "Fear God!"

"The fear of God" is the biblical language for what in our time passes for "being serious." But pay careful attention to the much loftier and more glorious meaning that this conveys.

A "serious person" is someone who is self-satisfied. They resist the dishonesty and scoffing emptiness of their surroundings. They oppose it and pursue what's better and more meaningful in life. They consider carefully what they're doing. They calculate the consequences. They're mindful of what people don't observe. But all of this happens in their own strength and through their own excellent qualities. In their own estimation, such people are part of a kind of moral aristocracy.

By contrast, "the fear of the Lord" cuts this Arminian thistle off at its roots. It humbles you to the dust along with all those scoffers. It makes you as guilty in the presence of the Holy One as all the mockers. It teaches you that all you do must be done meaningfully and evaluated meaningfully because God is secretly involved with all of it. You can never say about any of it: "This involves me alone, not God!"

The "serious person" sets the standards for their life and opposes everything that puts pressure on the rules they have made. But the God-fearing person bows before the law of God and moves forward with all God's people in the power of the atoning blood.

You can be "serious" and still essentially worship yourself. But "the fear of God" keeps on disturbing you until every idol in your life has been toppled.

A person can be "serious" even on their deathbed, from which they'll be carried off to hell. But "the fear of God" bears a person up on the glorious promise that shortly they will see "the secret things of God"!

So now you understand why people endeavor to be "serious" but avoid talking about "the fear of God."

Oh, all that chatter about "being serious" inflates the ego! It keeps alive the sense of self as we imagine it! But when the "fear of God" takes over, the entire creature is compelled to submit. The Lord lives and he alone is great.

The lesson to be learned from all of this is obvious.

We learn that "being serious" is an inferior concept. It does bear a nobler stamp when contrasted with the terribly harebrained approach to life in our age. And we also learn that Scripture talks to us not about "being serious" but about something much higher, holier, and more glorious. It uses the language of "fearing God." It obligates us Christians to recognize that fundamentally we are "not serious" and that we reject our Christian honor when we allow ourselves to be inspired by the spirit of the age rather than by God's Word. For then, in effect, we sever the nerve of "fearing God." What we're left with is merely "being serious"!

7 *You are a hiding place for me;*
you preserve me from trouble;
you surround me with shouts of
deliverance.

8 *I will instruct you and teach you in the*
way you should go;
I will counsel you with my eye upon
you.

9 *Be not like a horse or a mule, without*
understanding,
which must be curbed with bit and
bridle,
or it will not stay near you.

10 *Many are the sorrows of the wicked,*
but steadfast love surrounds the one
who trusts in the LORD.

11 *Rejoice in the* LORD *and be exalted, you*
righteous.
Sing for joy, you upright in heart.

11

UPRIGHT IN HEART

The most intense struggle that a child of the kingdom can experience is with unrighteousness.

I'm not talking about the everyday, external wickedness that consists of lying to or deceiving a neighbor. For those temptations as well as the inclination to all other sins are lodged in his wicked heart. But, schooled by the Word and Spirit to understand that lying and deception are works of the Devil, a person is able in the Lord's strength to abstain from such wanton service to the Devil. The Word commands this: "Let every man speak the truth to his neighbor." By the power of the Word, he does just that.

No, the insincerity with which a child of God struggles until the day they die goes much deeper. It's lodged inside and touches their spiritual standing before our All-Knowing God. That's why Almighty God, the Father of believers, says consistently: "Let me see that you walk before me sincerely." Psalm 25 says: "Let uprightness and godliness protect me." Christ was amazed to find that Nathaniel was a genuine person "without deceit. Truly, no deceit was found in him." And the great, glorious promise found in the New Testament is "that true worshipers will worship the Father in spirit and in truth."

The deeply insightful Psalm 32 provides light on the question of what the Lord God means by the uprightness of his children. The struggling person who by the Spirit's leading pours out their soul in this psalm is a child of God. But they're a child of God who deviates, struggles, and falls into sin. And now, after having fallen into sin, they find themself standing in God's presence as insincere. After they fell into sin, their heavenly Father sought them out. God scrutinized them with that holy, godly, penetrating look of his. By that look he intended to wound them as well as to connect with them.

But the fallen child of God didn't want to see that disturbing look on God's face. They didn't dare to return it. They didn't look up at their God looking down on them. And when they very clearly felt and understood that God wanted them to say something, they didn't say a word. They remained silent. This is how David put it: "When I stayed silent … your hand was heavy on me all day and all night. My strength was sapped, as in the heat of summer." But that silence was wrong on David's part, for in the immediately preceding verse he confesses that "my spirit was deceitful."

But then he comes clean and says very frankly that this was foolish on his part. He should have spoken immediately when God confronted him. He should have confessed his guilt. He acknowledges that he had been "like a horse or a mule, like an animal that has no understanding."

Of what benefit to him was it that he had been so insincere in God's presence? Did it help him at all? Did it remove his sin? Did it prevent God from knowing his sin? Was his soul uplifted a little by this silence of his, by his proud and arrogant silence?

Not at all! In fact, his heart languished. His soul was torn apart. He felt oppressed inwardly by it. It made him very tense to avoid looking his holy God in the eye! In fact, it made him miserable.

Just listen to his jubilation, however, when his soul finally broke through his silence: "Oh, how blessed when God forgives someone for their transgressions and covers their sins. How unspeakably blessed I am now that the Lord no longer counts my iniquities and that my heart is free of deceit." He had moved from death to life, from despair to joy.

But initially he had not wanted to have anything to do with that blessedness or with that amazing grace. He had spent the whole day, every day, making a lot of noise; but through all that clamor, his soul had remained totally silent. He had simply left God standing there, tested him, and held out on him. "But when I was silent," he confesses now, "my bones wasted away."

That's because opposing God and holding out on him causes us pain. It gnaws at the marrow of our bones.

Finally, he could hold out no longer. The large dike of his own pride was breached. The waters of God's grace flooded into the fields once again. "Then I made known my sins. I no longer concealed my unrighteousness. I said: 'I will speak; I will confess my transgressions to the Lord!' Oh, blessed experience! As soon as my confession crossed my lips, my faith was restored 'and you forgave my sin and unrighteousness.' "

Now set free, he is jubilant and he professes: "Therefore, all who are holy will worship you in the day they are found. And even a flood of great waters will not touch them!" Then he adds: "Rejoice in the Lord, O you righteous! Sing for joy, you upright in heart!"

Scripture itself teaches us what it means for God's children to be "upright in heart." It intends to say that they should not merely think: "God certainly knows what I've done wrong!" But they should remember that they are obligated and accountable to make known to

God themselves what their sins are. They're required to spell them out for him. They're obligated to confess them, not keep quiet about them. They're expected to do so continuously and to admit to suffering the deepest humiliation that a child of God can possibly endure with respect to the eternally merciful love of God.

And don't just say that all of this doesn't matter all that much, or that it will happen rather automatically. Don't think that pretty much everyone responds this way. The experience of the soul tells us just the opposite! It demonstrates that sin produces something quite different. It weakens and reduces the ability to pray. It sees to it that people really do want to drop to their knees, but that they seldom get around to it. It makes sure that when people pray, they pray in generalities. It guarantees that their praying lacks the moral power to force them beyond the outer court and into the holy of holies.

The destruction that sin produces is quite awful. Compare a bud on a stem that you think is going to open and blossom. Then sin comes along, and like a worm it chews on that stem. Before you know it, the bud that should have opened just withers away.

Ahhhhh! But there's still an enduring power of life remaining in the root! Sin no longer brings death to the plant cultivated by God, even though sometimes there's fear that it might. Grace, nothing but grace, is what finally turns the heart in a new direction. Heated passions die down in the heart. Calmness is restored. This is the sensibility brought by the soothing strokes of a higher hand. The soul that so recently was still angry and untrue shuts down to unrighteousness, and it no longer yearns for what it shouldn't. Then it opens and unfolds and emits a wonderful fragrance. From the depths it is now able to profess: "Father, I have sinned against heaven and against you. I am not worthy of being called your child." That's when it realizes once again that what it thought was gone was really present all along, namely, "the everlasting arms of mercy"!

Sisters and brothers, when your soul genuinely confesses your guilt, you are enabled to pour out your hearts to the Lord. But then never exalt in yourself. That you are able to do this, that you now feel that you're being completely truthful, and that this comes very easily for you is due only and completely to God's merciful grace!

This still needs to be added, however.

A child of God doesn't experience this struggle only in unusual spiritual circumstances. It doesn't happen only when they're dealing with a blatant sin that goes against their better judgment and is persistent and brutalizing.

The intense battle against wickedness needs to be waged constantly.

To suppose that there is as much as a single moment in their life while a child of God is here on earth when sin doesn't grate their soul is an abhorrent self-delusion. Sin oppresses them. It restricts their spiritual maturation. It puts them in tension with the image of the Son of God being renewed within them.

The person who judges casually imagines otherwise. But the person who uses a more exacting measurement knows better.

Look, sin produces inner discord. When we examine ourselves closely, very closely, we feel we're good for nothing. Everything about us falls away. We've nothing left to offer. And then the tempter whispers: "Is this really a child of the God who reigns on high?" And when the world comes along and regards us as being so much holier than we really are, or when Christian brothers and sisters see a holiness in us that really isn't there, then our hearts are split down the middle. Then there's a chasm between what's in our hearts and what crosses our lips! That distance is what's false, insincere, deceitful, and even self-deceitful, about us. It shouldn't exist. It has to be closed. "Lord, let my tongue and my mouth and the deepest desires of my heart be well-pleasing to you!"

To realize this, you need faith! You need faith to understand how miserable you are, how glorious Jesus is, and how richly merciful God is. With such faith, you will be able to see and understand and experience this truth: "The All-Merciful God has addressed my miserable condition from the riches that are in Christ Jesus."

Such faith is the ax wielded against the root of wickedness.

PSALM 41

1 *Blessed is the one who considers the poor!*
   In the day of trouble the Lord *delivers him;*
2 *the* Lord *protects him and keeps him alive;*
   he is called blessed in the land;
   you do not give him up to the will of his enemies.

3 **The** Lord **will support him on his sickbed.**
   In his illness, you will completely transform the bed on which he lies.

4 *As for me, I said, "O* Lord, *be gracious to me;*
   heal me, for I have sinned against you!"
5 *My enemies say of me in malice,*
   "When will he die, and his name perish?"

12

YOU COMPLETELY
TRANSFORM HIS ILLNESS

Our sick and afflicted!

What an overwhelming amount of quietly endured pain and hidden suffering lies hidden behind that expression "our sick and afflicted"! Other people don't much notice, but there's often a lot of fear behind that curtain. How many illusions are exploded in the rooms of the sick! How many flickering hopes extinguished! How many little flowers snapped off their stems! Add the actual pain that goes along with this. Pain that is very intense! Constant pain! Pain that never ends! Pain that burns so deep that it penetrates our bones! It's all covered up so well. The majority of people hardly take any notice of it at all. But for our sick it's a different matter. Theirs is a different kind of world, and you can safely say that it's a terrible world, at least as long as people endure their suffering without God.

Do you pay much attention to those who are sick? Are they a living part of your prayers? Aren't they confined pretty much to the formal prayers of the congregation, although with pity and compassion, when it meets on Sunday?

They are "our sick," and you have a sense of what that involves. They belong to us. They are part of our circles. They are part of our congregation. They have left our homes and gone to their sick rooms. They are our flesh and blood. Our sick are lying there in order to send us a message. They're there to appeal to us in our casual superficiality by in effect telling us: "It won't be long before you'll be where I am." Our sick became sick so that we may shower our love on them. So that our faith might be evident to them! So that we might comfort them by what we say to them! Our sick that are lying in front of us dressed in their white gowns are like priests and priestesses who whisper: "This is all because of our sinfulness, and that involves you too!" Yes, why should we be writing only about "our sick"? They are salt to us in our corrupt and corrupting lives. If sicknesses had not come into their lives, how many others would never have found God? How much devotion and self-denial would never have seen the light of day? How much more unrestrained would those who lightheartedly pursue worldly pleasures have been? Illnesses serve as a restraining grace in our circle of the living. And that's the glory associated with those who lie ill among us. They suppose that they are doing nothing, but they are actually blessing us! They imagine that all their suffering is useless, when in fact it strengthens the bonds holding the Lord's household together.

Amazing, isn't it? To prevent all supports from collapsing under the weight of material pursuits and superficial diversions, the Lord God sends an attacking angel. From its bowl of wrath, it sprinkles some drops on a dearly loved, rosy-cheeked child who becomes pale and wastes away. Next a few more fall on a pious child of God who is zealous for the Lord of Hosts but is suddenly blocked in the prime of life.

If there has to be sickness at all, you say to yourself, why doesn't God afflict the godless or the aged who are going to die anyway?

Naturally, as long as you think about being sick as a useless waste of time, it won't make any sense. But if you see it as a time when the power of the kingdom can be displayed, then it's something else again. For through sickness, God can bind the Devil's work in the social order and open up opportunities for the greatest tenderness. Then you understand how a sick person sometimes is far more useful and accomplishes more for the Lord than a person in full health. Then you can also see why God often allows so many of his dearest children to become ill. It's because they are the ones through whom he can do his best work. God's dear children always have other children of God who love them dearly. So the situation turns out beautifully. God's dear children are Satan's favorite target. For that reason, they carry a heavier obligation to guard their soul than other people do. It's also true that when they're sick in bed, things often turn out better for them than for children of the world. Rivet and Witsius were both highly learned professors. But they may well have contributed more to building the inner kingdom of God during the few days that they were sick in bed than they did through all their scholarly writing! We can't calculate that, of course, but the spiritual power of a God-glorifying sickbed stretches incredibly far! It's a spark that starts a fire and that in turn starts others generation after generation. It's a seed buried in the ground that always produces even more grain at the tip of the stalk when it ripens.

So now ask whether God is acting unjustly! Ask whether he is being unfair by causing his dearest children to suffer!

Well, remember Golgotha! "He laid on him the iniquity of us all! By his stripes we are healed!" Now you'd like to drop your question, wouldn't you?

But not so quickly! Show a little of Job's courage and like him tell your would-be comforter: "God's ways are not always easy! I will accuse the Almighty and make my case before him!" For there's a definite solution. And it's presented in the words of the psalmist at the beginning of these reflections.

No, the Lord God doesn't act unjustly when he lays suffering on his dearest children. For, in the words of David, the Spirit says: "In his illness, you will completely transform the bed on which he lies."

The God who possesses such mysterious powers deals freely with his dearest children. And what is the mystery involved in this "complete transformation"?

Isn't it the mystery of Marah? Early in its pilgrimage, Israel came to a well in the desert, but it could not drink the water because it was too bitter. Then Israel's shepherd called on the Lord, and the Lord showed him something. He threw it into the water, and what happened? The bitter water became sweet. Then Israel continued on its journey in the wilderness until it reached twelve springs of water and seventy palm trees. And it camped by those waters.

And precisely that is the sacred mystery involving God's dearest children when they make their way through the wilderness of life's illnesses. He completely changes everything for them.

Not always! Sometimes he goes away and leaves people alone. That could be because they don't love him or because he wants to test their love. That's when things get very bad and seethe in the depths of their soul. That's when dark clouds roil, and when sometimes just a brief flash of faith's lightening still pierces the gloom.

But that's not where things stay. After a shorter or longer time, the Lord returns. Then a miracle happens. Even if the condition remains unchanged or the illness perhaps becomes even worse and the oppressiveness more frightening, it no longer involves what it did before. "God has completely transformed the bed of illness on which the person lies!"

The bitterness remained, but yet it became sweet.

That's because the Lord came. He embraced the soul. He breathed strength into it. He brought the comfort of his most tender reassurances.

Then a journey of faith commences. Everything takes on a new appearance. The branches of the palms sway softly in the distance as they stand among the refreshing springs of water. That's where God's children make camp. The onlookers think: "How terrible! How bitterly painful!" But God's children take no notice. "They find that what has crossed their lips is sweet rather than bitter!"

What makes all the difference is whether a sickbed is endured with God or without him!

8 They say, "A deadly thing is poured out
on him;
  he will not rise again from where he
  lies."

9 Even my close friend in whom I trusted,
  who ate my bread, has lifted his heel
  against me.

10 But you, O LORD, be gracious to me,
  and raise me up, that I may repay
  them!

11 By this I know that you delight in me:
  my enemy will not shout in triumph
  over me.

12 **But as for me, you uphold me in my
  uprightness
  and you set me before your face forever.**

13 Blessed be the LORD, the God of Israel,
  from everlasting to everlasting!
    Amen and Amen.

13

YOU SET ME BEFORE
YOUR FACE FOREVER

Many apparently insignificant expressions over which a person reads quickly exist particularly in the book of Psalms. Yet, when a person plumbs their depths, they yield rich comfort and are a source of grace. That's true of the words from Psalm 41 that stand above this little meditation. Think into it for a minute and let it register on your soul. What wonderful grace is tucked away in those brief words!

I should have died, says the child of God, but I didn't! I will triumph over my enemy and over the man who torments my soul. But this certainly won't happen because I'm able to withstand him or because I'm stronger than he is. It will only be because I am a child of my God. It doesn't depend on me his child, but only on God! It's because the honor of my God and Father is involved. That's why, and for that reason alone, God's child ultimately perseveres, no matter how much unhappiness may be involved.

Ultimately getting through categorically doesn't happen without righteousness. Otherwise all the devils would raise objections and scream to high heaven from the depths of hell: "God is unrighteous!" And if things unfolded like that, the devils themselves would also find themselves in heaven!

No, God's child holds out with righteousness and without the least bit of unrighteousness. And the mystery of how that can happen the psalmist solves from his own spiritual experience. Again and again he resists clinging to his own righteousness, but he finds that God establishes that in him and for him. "Lord, as for me, you uphold me in my uprightness!" Uprightness! That's even more than righteousness, for in effect that amounts to saying: "I am made righteous by you, and I would never claim that I have gotten to that point by myself!" Uprightness confesses in and from the heart: "The Lord himself accomplished this, and he alone!"

And how does this work of his unfold?

Very simply said, my good brother and sister, it is accomplished because God in his love does one very simple thing: he "sets you before his face forever."

He did that in eternity and before laying the foundations of the world. In that act of setting someone before his face forever, both your election and the root of your salvation in that election are bound together.

"Setting you before his face" also included your regeneration by infusing your soul with the capacity to believe when you were brought to life from death. Recognize that all of your worldly living and abiding in death amounted to standing outside of his light and happened because you were estranged from him, your God. Your awakening to new life through faith was precisely your coming to stand before God's face and immediately seeing by the light of his presence both your eternal death and the unfathomable depth of his grace. And this much you know for certain, that you did not go and stand before God's face! He was the one who placed you there!

Oh, the divine moment of your eternal rebirth, when the All-Compassionate God looked down on you. Then it became impossible for you ever to leave him, for now you were positioned in his presence, standing before his awesome and yet so reassuring face.

And is that the way it's always going to be?

For you and I remained so ungodly that after his miraculous work of mercy and after briefly enjoying our presence before him, we suddenly decided that a person is not capable of looking upon God continually. Our souls told us that we had had enough of God and that there was not a lot of life in such a monotonous existence. We wanted to get back to what was really visible. Naturally, we did this with the idea that later we could return to God. But for the moment, at least, we were going to enjoy something good away from him. But in turning away from him, we really wanted to do so while still singing: "Yet it's really good, it's a source of blessing to me, to be near to my God!"

Truly, how perplexing our human hearts actually are! We really scare ourselves sometimes, don't we?

But the fact is, a child of God can't have or do what they want. They may want to run away from God in order to be free, but God doesn't let them do this. All the running away happens only in a dream. They imagine that they're out of God's presence. They picture themselves as now being free. They dream that later they'll go back to God. But in reality, all of this is nothing more than a mirage.

They simply can't! For God has "set them before his face forever"! At best, they can only touch their lips to the cup of sin before a terrifying light shines all around them and a fire burns inside them. So what is this heaviness of conscience? This sadness pouring over their souls? That terrible weakness in their legs? What else is it but the face of God, in whose presence you are standing forever? That's the reason why a child of God can't sin without the sinning being followed by terrible turmoil in the soul and soul-wrenching remorse.

But remorse is followed by praise. For God always succeeds. If you humble yourself and cry out with a submissive heart: "O God, just give up on me. I don't deserve to lift my eyes and look you in the face!" then God always does the same thing. He sets you before his face once again. But now it's before his comforting face, and the love of Christ begins flowing quietly into your heart.

And so, God be praised, that's how it will be forever. "You set me before your face forever." That's why, whatever may come and whatever may threaten us, we are never overcome by it, and it always turns out well. For God is God. And when we are once above, all desire to be away from God will be gone, because that's how our own wills will forever want it. Then God will place all his children before his face to enjoy his everlasting presence. Jehovah exalted in his saints!

Oh, may his mercy grant this glory also in you and me!

5 Behold, I was brought forth in iniquity,
  and in sin did my mother conceive me.
6 Behold, you delight in truth in the
  inward being,
    and you teach me wisdom in the secret
    heart.
7 Purge me with hyssop, and I shall be
  clean;
    wash me, and I shall be whiter than
    snow.
8 Let me hear joy and gladness;
    let the bones that you have broken
    rejoice.
9 Hide your face from my sins,
    and blot out all my iniquities.

**10 Create in me a clean heart, O God.
And renew a steadfast spirit in my
inmost parts.**

11 Cast me not away from your presence,
    and take not your Holy Spirit from me.
12 Restore to me the joy of your salvation,
    and uphold me with a willing spirit.

14

RENEW A STEADFAST SPIRIT IN MY INMOST PARTS!

Not everyone knows about so-called spiritual conflict. And those who actually are involved with struggles of the soul have experienced for many years already that all this talk about "spiritual heavyheartedness" actually amounts to nothing more than pious fanaticism.

This situation can be explained by the fact that in the natural order of things, there is no inherent conflict between Satan and our hearts. If we begin with the fact that we are friends of Satan, how could we ever be his enemies? No, the conflict arises because God does what he promised in Genesis 3:15 that he would do: "I will put enmity between … " If the conflict between us and Satan existed naturally, then God would not have had to promise that he would put enmity between the two of us. So now we are by nature friends of this world and enemies of God. Consequently, it's obvious that a real miracle has to occur within us to turn this situation completely around! That miracle has to create a situation in our lives in which we become enemies of Satan and friends of God!

And when it once gets to that point in our lives, then the battle, the spiritual conflict, the wrestling of the soul becomes automatic. Not immediately at full strength! Not with equal strength for everyone! Here much depends on you personally, on your personal circumstances, and on your past. But once it does get to that point, everyone experiences this struggle. And once the battle begins, it doesn't stop until we enter our eternal rest. This is a battle not first of all against people whose thinking is different from our own or against worldly society. These actually have nothing to do with this spiritual struggle. But this is a battle that is fought in our inmost parts. In the hidden recesses of our hearts! Deep inside our souls, where no other person can detect what's going on there! On the distant horizons of our innermost emotional lives, where we discover our inner evil and corruption! Where our secret sins are found on which the Lord shines the light of his presence! On those concealed compromises that likely even our closest and dearest friends here on earth don't know about!

The battle rages between the Holy Spirit and Satan over us. As a result, it is also a battle between our own faith fostered by the Holy Spirit and our own wicked heart, behind which Satan hunkers down.

The faith in us is a new, sacred power that has been placed within us. It clings tightly to the Messiah, strives toward God, and does not abandon the Holy Spirit. Accordingly, it regularly and squarely opposes all the wicked, sinful, and godless desires that arise within us. Believing and yearning are the sharp instruments with which this battle is conducted. Originally everything was captured in a single desire. Then the law said: "You shall not covet!" But that didn't stop you! On the contrary! Desiring agitated you all the more intensely, adding fuel to the fires burning in your desires. And that's where things stayed until God created faith within you. And that faith, as you know, was something different, something contrary, and something that militated against your desiring. And that's how spiritual struggle began.

The battle did not consist of putting a stop to desiring and beginning to believe. Then no spiritual struggle would have occurred at all. No, desire continued. It even became stronger than it had been. And that's precisely what caused your inner wrestling, surprised you about your soul, and produced your heavyheartedness.

Now it wasn't Satan who was doing the yearning, but you were doing the coveting. Now it wasn't the Holy Spirit who was doing the believing in and for you, but you were doing the believing. It's true, the coveting did not originate with you, but Satan worked it in you. But it's also true that the fruit that this bore was that you yourself, personally, in your self-centeredness became a covetous person. And at the same time, faith did not originate with you either. The Holy Spirit worked it in you. But it's also true that its fruit was that you yourself, personally, in the core of your being became a believing person. Don't vacillate on this! Hold on to it resolutely. You are a being who yearns and one who believes. It's from the two of these that your inner spiritual struggle arises. This is a conflict not at the place you work. Not in the circles of people where you live and interact! Not even in your emotions! No, it's a conflict that occurs in that most deeply hidden part of you, deep inside you, in what David in Psalm 51 calls his "inmost parts" when he says: "Renew a steadfast spirit in my inmost parts." It happens in what we often refer to as our "ego." That's where the mystery is concealed. That ego is dead, because Paul states: "It is no longer I that live." And yet, that ego enters into the most glorious life imaginable, for the same apostle also says: "What lives in me is that I live through faith in the Son of God!"

What proceeds from that inmost core of our egos is a dynamic influence on every dimension of our soul's existence: on our imagination, on our emotions, and on our will. And what this dynamic influence on our ego produces in our imagination, emotions, and will is our spirit. It is the spirit of our humanity within us.

That spirit participates in the conflict going on within our inner selves. In the mysterious vacillation between longing and believing two frequently opposing dynamics are at work on this spirit of ours. If faith is busy working in the core of our being, well then, the strength of faith exerts a holy power on our imagination, our emotions, and our will so that they become instruments of righteousness. By the same token, if the force of longing is at work in us, then the power of sin exerts a sinful force on our spirit, and our imagination, our emotions, and our will become instruments of unrighteousness.

If that back-and-forth dynamic is exerting pressure so that now faith is working more powerfully and then it almost completely disappears and a powerful, terrible sense of yearning prevails, then the spiritual battle within us is at its most intense.

But God's long-suffering and his mercies toward us are great. Through his Holy Spirit he diverts and renders ineffective the depth of these powerful, natural desires. He causes our faith to work powerfully and consistently for a time. But then a moment comes once again when the dynamic is reversed and the power of yearning unexpectedly overwhelms us. It is turned loose and prevails. Then it enlists those parts of our being in the service of unrighteousness.

Then our soul mourns deeply, sadly.

And those dimensions of the ego thought: "Now I've arrived! Things have gone very well for so many days and weeks. Finally, after all this time, God in his mercy has heard me and broken the power of sin." But watch out! That's when you lose everything once again!

How can that happen? How else than because when things were finally going so well, you stopped being watchful. It happened when you actually began imagining that your faith is a sure thing! You no longer took it hour by hour, bit by bit. You no longer thought of it as a gift from the loving hand of your Father in heaven.

And that had to be punished. That's the reason, the only reason, that the Lord God turned you loose! He didn't fail you. That wasn't the cause of letting go of you. But it was for sinning with respect to your believing that he, the Holy God, was punishing you.

But he who punishes is also vigilant. He sees to it that the wounds that he had to inflict on you do not cause you to bleed to death!

And thus, while the punishment has not yet ended, the dynamic that turns you back to him begins working again. Faith begins functioning once more. A deep, soul-wrenching sorrow develops. Clinging to the all-sufficient blood of the Lamb is restored. A sense of your poor, naked, empty-handed dependence and smallness returns. You become meek and lowly once more, and God renews his grace to you.

Now the soul lives again, and prays again. But now it still doesn't pray with the same strength or earnestness or forcefulness that it had when it prayed: "Lord, create in me a steadfast spirit."

That vacillation now becomes the source of deep sadness where God is concerned. Initially a person didn't have much interest in this swinging back and forth. But now it has become a curse on the soul.

Initially it had the attitude: "Oh, if God would only sanctify my spirit, I'll see to it that it stays steadfast!" But that has changed. Languishing in the awareness of its own impotence, it now prays: "O Lord God, I'm not able to do this by myself! In your mercy, create in me a steadfast spirit."

14 Deliver me from bloodguiltiness, O God,
  O God of my salvation,
  and my tongue will sing aloud of your
  righteousness.
15 O Lord, open my lips,
  and my mouth will declare your
  praise.
16 For you will not delight in sacrifice, or I
  would give it;
  you will not be pleased with a burnt
  offering.

**17 The sacrifices of God are a broken spirit;
a broken and contrite heart you,
O God, will not despise.**

18 Do good to Zion in your good pleasure;
  build up the walls of Jerusalem;
19 then will you delight in right sacrifices,
  in burnt offerings and whole burnt
  offerings;
  then bulls will be offered on your altar.

15

BROKENHEARTED

To be "brokenhearted," if you really think about it, is really the most difficult demand that can be laid on a sinful human being.

To be curbed a little isn't objectionable to our big egos. You hardly ever come across someone who won't acknowledge that they don't fail sometime and at some things. Everyone acknowledges that they could do better than they sometimes do. As long as there's talk about nothing worse than curbing a person's lavish excesses, you're not going to get an actual objection from most of them.

That kind of curtailed person walks around by the thousands on the biblical broad road, strutting their restraint and modesty. Hemmed in by the fences of their own self-righteousness, they live and work in their own kind of hell.

But that doesn't matter to God. It doesn't matter to him in his mysterious judgment as long as his light penetrates and exposes what's going on.

But as far as the Searcher of every heart is concerned, you don't make a lick of progress by punishing, curbing, subduing, and if necessary even cracking and breaking your bodily members. Every child of God knows the failed track record here.

But things can't stay like this. The sails of sinful living have to be trimmed. It has to be reined in. The body has to be forcibly subdued. But people don't want to do this any longer. And this will destroy them. It will kill them. Sins, to be specific, need to be rendered ineffective. Things that appealed to people before no longer do. Change is noticeable. Progress is being made. And this amounts to more than merely curbing. It consists of circumcising the old, wild nature.

And yet this does not get you to where you should be. It can't. For however much you mutilate your way of living, this is not yet taking a stand against it. Then you're simply replacing the natural leg you amputated with a wooden one, or if necessary, with a crutch, and you keep on stumbling along in your old ways with artificial support! Oh, even mutilated spiritual strugglers are under the constraints of hell.

No, our physical members behave like unchecked growth. They are untamed sucker shoots in daily living. When it comes to dealing with God, you have to deal with life itself. The divine medical doctor doesn't just examine your foot or your hand. He examines everything. Even what's beneath your clothing! Right down to your heart! And he doesn't hesitate or doubt for a second. He talks straight from the shoulder! Man-to-man! "This heart has to change!"

Listen closely! Objections arise immediately to that diagnosis by the Lord our God: "My heart can't handle that! I'd die if I tried. I live by what's in my heart. Test me! Take everything else, O divine physician, but don't let the scalpel of your Word cut into my heart. Take this hand; here, I offer it to you! Take that leg; I can do without it! Just let me keep on creeping along and stumbling forward. I'm willing to do anything to be saved. I'm ready for anything. No pain frightens me, no matter how intense it might be. But whoever heard of a person having to give up their heart? That they had to cut it out? That they had to crush it to a pulp? How could anyone endure that kind of procedure and remain alive?"

With talk like that, the willful, self-righteous heart bent on protecting itself reappears!

But no, O Lord my God, I will not withhold even my heart from you. Even my heart needs to be changed! It is too arrogant. It needs to be humbled. My heart and my will truly do want to bow before you!

But God in his holiness remains adamant.

But no, emphatically not! A yielded heart is still not enough! The promise of salvation is held out only to a broken heart. A yielded heart doesn't matter, because in the first place it just doesn't go far enough. It's still too inflexible. Even if it might bend over and bow down today, tomorrow it will snap right back up. And that amounts to only playing games with the Almighty. That's dealing in appearances, not inner truth.

That's why not a jot or tittle of God's Word can be changed! Broken! Really broken! Shattered to pieces in the full sense of the word! That's what has to happen to your arrogant and resistant heart.

"But ... then it's all over for me. Then I'd stop existing. That amounts to dying!"

That's definitely the case, my good readers. That's what it's all about. And that's exactly why it has to be as stated. Your heart has to be broken. You have to die. You have to stop living for what's in your old heart. Because if you really do get to that point, then you won't die, but you'll start living again!

There's room for everything else in hell. Just not for a broken human heart!

When living for self disappears in brokenheartedness, that's the precise moment when living in Jesus begins.

In the instant that you lance a vein and drain the bad blood of living for self, the life-giving blood of Jesus flows into your soul.

This is why the text uses the word "broken." "A broken heart!" A heart shattered to pieces! A brokenness that endures until the heart lies in smithereens!

This doesn't happen all at once. For some people the hammer of his Word pounds on the rock pile of their heart for years.

First he trims a little. Then he cuts more deeply. Then he applies more pressure on you. He sends judgments that frighten you, and he compels you to take swallow after swallow from the chalice of his fury. His intent is to oppress your soul.

Your joy flees. Your favorite plaything is gone. Your circle of friends melts away. Every night you long for the morning. Every aspiration is dashed.

That's when every crushed person weeps and laments, complaining: "The world doesn't offer me a thing anymore." They feel like adding: "This last blow has simply broken my heart!"

Then God answers: "No, no, no! What broke in you is only what you imagined to be the love and hope of your heart! Your heart itself is intact!" And now the real spiritual work begins. Blow after blow was the tugging of a higher hand within you. Blow after blow was the prodding of your soul. Blow after blow was the pounding of God's hammer, his Word, on different parts of your heart.

That's what happens to the idol Dagon. An arm comes off. A foot falls off. Finally the whole idol is cut in half, its proud bearing devastated. And God keeps hammering on it until its will, its emotions, its honor, its self-worth, its virtue, and its piety, even its praying and charitable giving, all lie in the dust, pulverized at God's feet.

When that happens, a miracle occurs. When Dagon has been toppled, the godless ego is rendered impotent. Everything that was our pride and strength lies there as pulverized dust. But lo and behold, in the same heart where Dagon lies dashed to pieces, Someone else, Someone better has forced his way in!

Don't you know him?

He's your Savior. "Comforter" is his name!

5 But God will break you down forever;
    he will snatch and tear you from your
    tent;
    he will uproot you from the land of the
    living.
6 The righteous shall see and fear,
    and shall laugh at him, saying,
7 "See the man who would not make
    God his refuge,
    but trusted in the abundance of his
    riches
    and sought refuge in his own
    destruction!"

8 **I am like a green olive tree
in God's house.
I rely on God's mercy now
and for eternity.**

9 I will thank you forever,
    because you have done it.
    I will wait for your name, for it is good,
    in the presence of the godly.

16

LIKE A GREEN OLIVE
TREE IN GOD'S HOUSE

C hrist is living! And the life of our Lord Jesus Christ
is a continuous source of the power of life flowing,
pouring from it. This power pervades everything. It is
not limited by distance, but it springs from the heart of
Jesus and is here on earth in a split second. It is present in
your daily activities, your home, the privacy of your own
bedroom, and at the doorway of your heart. It is a power
that searches for you and does not give up until it finds
you. It always ends either with you crushing and discard-
ing it or by getting through to you. The latter is absolutely
wonderful! For then it permeates you, inspires you, exalts
you, sustains you, and roots you in the life of God himself.

All the glory of his church, all the preeminence his
people may possess, and all the strength of his elect are
rooted in the living Christ.

His church receives nothing at all from a dead Christ,
or even an unemployed Christ who is now seated somewhere high above us in heaven and is so far away from us
that we have to shout to him and hardly get back as much

as a faintly whispered answer. That's when the church is like a lamp without oil, a streambed without water, a parched skeleton without marrow or nerves.

When seen without the steady outpouring and infusion of Jesus' life-giving power, his church, every one of his elect people, and even your own heart are all no more than dead, shriveled carcasses. They are devoid of life's glow and inner appeal. They are worthless, good for nothing, and like a diamond in pitch-black darkness.

But that's not the case, praise God! The Son of God, our glorious Head, is never absent from us in his majesty or with his grace and his Spirit. The diamond is never without bright light shining on it. The root is filled with sap. The streambed is always brimming with flowing water. This is the case even when the church thinks it has no energy and vitality left at all. It's the case when an elect child of the Lord feels worthless and gives up. But that's when the living Christ comes to them, inspires them, and upholds them. That's when he speaks sacred, splendid words to them: "I'll be with you all the days of your life, even until the end of the world!"

This is not what the soul senses, however. It rarely has experiences like that. It's only been able to examine them a few times. If we had to rely on religious experience, we'd have to complain: "The Lord is absent from me three hundred days of the year! And it's already saying too much if I said that on the rest of them I only detect him from a long way off!"

If a gospel had to be fashioned on the basis of the religious experience of God's children, it would go like this: "Those who are superficial glory in their impression that Jesus is always with them. But those who reflect more deeply know that he has visited them on only a few occasions, and then only to spend the night!"

This is precisely the reason why God the Holy Spirit hasn't left the writing of the gospel up to us. That's why he did it himself. Thanks to that divine decision, what we have in his Word is not what we think about Jesus. We have him there as he really is. This is the Jesus presented to God's children there. He is the Jesus who has received all power in heaven and on earth. He is the divine Immanuel. And yet, he is also our brother. He is the Jesus who is ever living, always working, and continuously causing his power to flow from him. He is the Jesus who is always close to his church. He is always enlivening the souls of his elect, even when they take no notice of it.

On that basis, a child of God dares to exalt even during times when they feel abandoned. They exalt as David did when everything seemed lost, all hope was gone, he was walled off from everything, and the Holy Spirit enabled him not to complain even then: "I won't go down that road, but I will exalt and rejoice. 'I will be like a green olive tree in God's house, always and forever.' "

To speak such heroic words at such times is not based on mere religious experience but on a deep faith. It's a faith that relies on a God who is with us even when he doesn't seem to be. It's a faith that calls out to him as though he is present.

An olive tree! I'm an olive tree! That is, I'm such a precious plant that I never shrivel but always stay green. I'm a tree on which people see no fruit from a distance, but when they shake me, the little olives rain down on them on all sides. I'm a tree beautiful in every way, and even my shape is enchantingly beautiful. I'm a tree whose chopped wood—although that's a very displeasing thought—even has a soft, lovely appearance.

That's the kind of olive tree, says David, that I'll be in the house of the Lord. It won't be standing alone on some naked rock like a one-eyed king. It won't be in the desert, where some brushwood passes for a tree. No, it will stand in the most splendid, beautiful courtyard of God's dwelling. It will be in that garden where the cedars and palm trees are on display and where the martyrs' descendants are nourished by their blood. It will be in that magnificent spiritual court where the selection of all the specimens has been coordinated. That's where I'll be, always green, green forever, the shoot of an olive! That's what David dared to exalt in at the very moment that everything seemed lost, when men were hunting him like the gazelle, and when Satan was attacking his sinful heart with thoughts of Nabal and Bathsheba.

So tell me. Do you understand now what the inspiration of sacred Scripture is all about?

It comes down to this. David himself did not really, truly know who he was. But the Holy Spirit did. And here the Holy Spirit is speaking for David. David repeats what he said. David believed what he said. And by means of that faith, David knew that he was God's child. That's how he moved beyond his sin and the shriveling of his soul. That's how he knew he was actually an olive tree, green on the inside. That's how he knew that such green growth didn't come from within himself but that it came from the ever-living Immanuel, who fashioned a greening olive tree from a parched David.

But what about you?

Are things any different for you?

Do you think you can really build anything on the basis of your religious experience?

Do you understand how matters stand with you? Do you know your own situation?

My dear sisters and brothers, consider those who are sick. So many who are sick actually feel very healthy. Their doctor just shakes his head knowingly. Feelings can really fool you!

On the other hand, there are a great many sick people who think they're not going to make it through the night. They are that deathly afraid. But their doctor tells them: "Don't worry. You're going to be fine!" It's only their imagination that threatens them.

And this is exactly how things are in that enormous hospital for souls. Only the Holy Spirit, the Great Physician, actually knows our condition. Our own feelings are misleading.

For that reason, the person who feels good shouldn't celebrate all that much. The person who doesn't shouldn't complain all that much, either.

But even when things are dark and bleak in your soul, believe him when the Holy Spirit comes to you and says: "The battle's over!" Simply respond: "O Holy Spirit, I really do believe you." Stammer the way David did, and confess that you are like "an olive tree in God's house, green now and green forever"!

PSALM 58

3 The wicked are estranged from the
womb;
    they go astray from birth, speaking
    lies.
**4 They are like a deaf viper
that has clogged its ears,**
5 so that it does not hear the voice of
charmers
    or of the cunning enchanter.
6 O God, break the teeth in their mouths;
    tear out the fangs of the young lions,
    O Lord!
7 Let them vanish like water that runs
away;
    when he aims his arrows, let them be
    blunted.
8 Let them be like the snail that dissolves
into slime,
    like the stillborn child who never sees
    the sun.
9 Sooner than your pots can feel the heat
of thorns,
    whether green or ablaze, may he
    sweep them away!

17

LIKE A DEAF VIPER

H oly Scripture everywhere displays great courage with respect to God's holiness. God himself dares to speak out against proud and important people in an effort to humble or break them so they fall on their faces. He neither spares them nor is intimidated by their position in life.

Thus, also here in Psalm 58, God addresses the sinner and says: "Actually, seen for what you are, you are no more than a deaf viper."

A viper!

It's a nasty, repulsive animal that automatically causes revulsion. People avoid it. They warn their children about it, telling them: "Don't touch it!" "A brood of vipers" is the harsh, sharp, cutting expression that Jesus used in striking back at the Pharisees and unmasking them. "The human heart is cunning and deadly; who can know it?" exclaims the prophet.

And here in this context the psalmist says that the ungodly person is "a viper" that spews out their poison. Behind their fangs is a venom that wounds and kills when they strike. Note well that this viper is not limited to an intentional deceiver, a thoroughly evil person, or a perverse corruptor of other souls. Not at all! It is saying that every person, every sinner, whether they do so willingly or unwillingly, can do nothing except corrupt the hearts of others. They incite those around them. They become a source of moral and spiritual death to them.

To do so, you don't only have to talk about or do wicked things. But your mere presence, your personality, and your unwitting way of living have a polluting effect. They have an evil effect and nurture evil in others.

Just as a viper can poison you regardless of whether it does so intentionally in order to protect itself or whether it does so merely instinctively, the result is the same. It doesn't think about whether the poison it spews lands on the grass and ground or is injected into your hand or arm. The same is true of what emanates from the sinner, whether it's their breath, their language, the fire in their eyes, their example, or their influence. So much of what comes from the poisonous glands of their own hearts never has a cleansing effect but has damaging results. When it goes to work, it produces death.

Now, it's the case that God has medicine, an antidote, for that poison that you spew on other people. It's comparable to the pharmaceutical measures that our medical doctors have at their disposal. They take poisonous materials, including snake venom, and have the knowledge of how to use these with certain diseases and under specific circumstances to counteract illness with a healing rather than destructive effect. Naturally, this doesn't change in the least the deadly nature of the venom itself. Nor does this detract at all from the evil nature of what is generated spiritually by you.

For you the concern is not what God may do with the poison you generate. Rather, it should be what effect you have on others. Is it a healthy or destructive influence?

The Holy Spirit confronts that very question here through the mouth of David. He applies it to the ungodly person who is unregenerate. But he applies it as well to the regenerate individual to the extent that they often fall out of fellowship with their Savior and then generate from the cells and glands of their soul only what is impure, sensuous, and poisonous.

It's very obvious that the evil is worse and that they are more accountable for it when people express it by choice, like the viper does in striking intentionally either by defending itself or by attacking. Then people exhibit a lust for evil. They behave with such premeditated counsel that evil bursts out of their souls' glands and splatters over others, infecting their lifeblood.

Now we're dealing with full-blown wickedness! Now an unholy force has power over our souls! Now we are not merely unwitting instruments but fully aware servants of unrighteousness. And that's much worse!

Even then, the fullest measure of corruption has not yet been reached. The worst is what is unique to us as sinners, and this goes far beyond what is found in an angry viper. Isaiah says emphatically that a person is not only like a viper, but that "your work is still worse than that of the viper" (41:24).[1] And the most revolting thing about what is worst is stated here in what the psalmist says in the verse I have quoted, namely, that people are not just vipers but especially that they are often like "deaf vipers"!

The animal that we identify as a viper can be charmed. There is a power in the human voice that, well developed for that purpose, has power over wild, poisonous animals. Particularly in the Orient in former times, the human voice was well developed, and people mastered the art of mesmerizing, so-called charming, and controlling snakes and other poisonous creatures.

---

1. English translations do not use "viper" here; Kuyper reflects the Dutch translation.

Applying this to people, a person could say that a certain power exists in God's voice that has the capability of subduing the viper in our soul. It can render it so powerless that it becomes incapable of spewing out poison. It is disarmed, and its capacity to inflict damage disappears. God's Word can be seen as a charm that casts a spell over the inner threats of the human soul.

While a viper or a snake is never deaf and is incapable of clogging its ears and is always definitely rendered powerless when it hears the soothing voice of its charmer, that's not true of people. Sinners, you and I and everyone else born by and in sin, frequently know how to play the part of a deaf viper. We know how to close our ears to the Word of God! And in speaking to our souls here, this is precisely what the Holy Spirit addresses and reproves in the remarkable image of the deaf viper. He's not just addressing a viper who is capable of spewing poisonous venom but especially one that is deaf to its divine charmer! He desires to disarm the viper within us by his amazingly miraculous Word.

That's why we can do no better than to understand how to expunge the poisonous fluids from our corrupt hearts. Nothing helps do this better in this regard than our full, totally enthusiastic confession of faith in Christ.

And things will not be as they should be with us until we willingly draw every drop of life-giving fluid that nourishes us and those around us from him who is the Spring and Fountain of Living Waters.

7 On God rests my salvation and my
glory;
  my mighty rock, my refuge is God.
8 Trust in him at all times, O people;
  pour out your heart before him;
  God is a refuge for us.

9 Common people are a mere puff of air
and important people are a lie.
Weighed together on a scale,
they amount to less than a breath.

10 Put no trust in extortion;
  set no vain hopes on robbery;
  if riches increase, set not your heart
  on them.
11 Once God has spoken;
  twice have I heard this:
  that power belongs to God,
12 and that to you, O Lord, belongs
  steadfast love.
  For you will render to a man
  according to his work.

18

IMPORTANT PEOPLE
ARE A LIE!

Y es, there definitely are important people here on earth. It's playing games to think that all people here on earth are the same. The children of human parents just are not! Among one another, they are very unequal. At the same time, everyone has to agree that the distinctions among them are so endlessly varied that any attempt to classify them is really quite lame. Yet, the people in the world around us noticeably fall into either an immeasurable mix of common ones or a small class of important ones.

They are regarded as common or important according to the standards of measurement that have always been applied and are still used. Common people have very little wealth, but important people have a great deal. Common ones have very little power, while important ones have a lot of it. Commoners have limited intellectual capacities, but prominent folks possess a great deal of thinking ability. Little people hardly matter in society, while big shots control it. Energy and willpower are in short supply among common people, but important people have them in epic proportions. Dependence is the norm for one, dominance for the other. Here a countless mass of the weak and vulnerable look at the limited number of important people in awe and amazement. They in return are scarcely inclined to even notice the ones to whom little has been given. The important and the common people represent the undeniable, enduring distinction that cuts through and divides all facets of human life.

The very few are the ones who accomplish something significant. They have the treasure and power, the talent and the drive, the influence and the control over the opportunities to do so. They make a name for themselves by doing so. They leave their footprints on the life of their community, city, country, and church. These people are surrounded by an ocean of what the psalmist calls "common people," who endlessly beat against them like the waves of the sea. These are the ordinary folks who are weaker and poorer. They are powerless and lack the genius and money of the others. They haven't been granted the same talent, resolve, and persistence. All they can do is huddle together as the masses, find solace in their numbers, and undertake in their strength what they realistically dare to do.

These important people are traveling in circumstances that are extremely dangerous for them. "It is easier for a camel to pass through the eye of a needle than for a rich man to enter the kingdom of God," said our Savior. But no one should think that this applies only to those who are rich in terms of money. Sadly, no! This is equally true, and perhaps even more frighteningly so, for those who are rich in genius, knowledge, determination, or social influence. Pay close attention to how few important people enter through the narrow gate. Also notice how many of those who give the appearance of entering actually remain behind. This even applies to preachers! In every century, they have been numbered among the important people in the church of Jesus Christ. They were the powerful. They had the authority. Yet how rarely hasn't there been a time when Chrysostom's complaint was echoed with his burning intensity: "Most shepherds are standing outside the sheepfold of Christ!"

It can't be any different! It's almost impossible even for ordinary, weak, and helpless people to discount themselves. How terribly more difficult, then, it must be for the very few who are celebrated, important, rich, powerful, and influential! They don't only have to deal with their own egos, but they also have to deny all the incense offered to them, all their influence, and their public image. With God all things are possible, but without it one of these prominent people could never enter God's glorious kingdom. It's like it is with the beauty of a woman! What a miracle of divine grace has to happen to cause a beautiful young daughter not to be held at bay from God by her beauty and not to be seduced by her vanity. Who wouldn't admit this?

There are so few important people here on earth who will also be great in the kingdom of heaven. They are inwardly so small. "They are a lie," says the psalmist. You could even say: "It's a lie that they are important." They definitely seem to be. But they really aren't. Those who are truly important possess inner depth. They are significant in the sight of God and will be so eternally. You will find them much more often among those who are poor. They are poor in terms of money, material goods, genius, and power. "Blessed are the poor in spirit, for theirs is the kingdom of heaven." "Unless you become like a little child, O you who are important here on earth, your portion in Jesus will disappear!"

But it's not only that the important people are traveling in circumstances that are dangerous for themselves. They are dragging common people into danger along with them. They have such enormous influence and power that people can't resist them. When the power of money or personality or reason are so ungodly that they only serve egoism, then that miserable influence becomes very oppressive and domineering for common people. Fear arises. Then fear becomes oppressiveness that gives way to cowardly flight or creeping bitterness. You can see in the life of a village how pernicious the power of an influential man can be on the lives of common people. If it comes to that kind of expression on the village level, how much worse it will be in the cities. Our world and our hearts are so sinful that every powerful person, who is no more than a sinner among sinners, is dangerous!

When a powerful person is not against you but is for you, they are especially dangerous. That's true if they help or bolster and support you. Just take a look around you in your surroundings. Notice the powerful people among you who pose a double danger. They cause you to depend too much on them. And they lean too heavily on your enthusiastic amazement regarding them. This is how the idols of this world appear. It's how their little altars are erected. It's how people then light incense to them. It's how honor for the Lord disappears and how powerful people are corrupted.

The spirit of the age nurtures this terrible evil very strongly. It does so even among Christians. It is intent on gaining ground on the false premise that important and powerful people attain personal recognition and make a name for themselves because of what they are in and of themselves.

This is why we need God's Word so much. It's the Word that also lays down a premise where important people are concerned. It's the theory that asserts exactly the opposite. It's the affirmation that is a source of comfort to the weak, of salvation for those who are important, and of honor to God. It endures century after century. It is the affirmation that the church of Christ continues to make: "Important people are not what you think they are; they are a lie!"

For if I'm a weak, common person and if I believe that the important people are a lie, then fear naturally subsides in my heart. Then I begin to live again. I dare to breathe and celebrate in my soul. One thing have I heard. The Lord told it to me twice, namely, that strength belongs to God; it is not lodged in powerful people.

This is what likewise saves those important folks. For something happens to an important person who knows and believes and comprehends that they "are a lie," that is, that it's simply not true that they are someone special. Then that temptation loses its appeal. Its power is broken. They accept the fact that they are no different from the least of all persons and that they are only an instrument in the service of the Lord God. They can humbly kneel before God again, creep toward him, and squeeze through the narrow gate.

This is how God reclaims his glory in the lives of powerful people. These important people are the works of his hands. He has fashioned them. They are his instruments. Just as a blacksmith wields a huge hammer to bend and shape the metal on his anvil, so God Almighty has several powerful hammers in addition to his more refined tools. They are available for him to use. But they lie idle and powerless in the corner until he extends his strong arm, grips them, and uses them to strike the red-hot metal he's shaping.

If the hammer would say: "I'm the blacksmith," it would be lying. But if that huge hammer remained a passive tool and recognized that God is the smith who's doing the work, it would be truthful. And that's the truth by which God is shaping his church.

And this explains how sometimes people of noble birth appear who are "important individuals" among the people but who are "very common men and women" in God's presence. That's to say, you can find children of God who are simultaneously powerful people in their generation here on earth and who are also great in the kingdom of heaven.

These would include the holy apostles, the martyrs, and the church's giants. They were important people who began by regarding themselves as "a lie," but who became the truth in him who "for our sakes became a worm and no man at all."

16 Why do you look with hatred, O many-
   peaked mountain,
      at the mount that God desired for his
      abode,
      yes, where the LORD will dwell forever?
17 The chariots of God are twice ten
   thousand, thousands upon thousands;
      the Lord is among them; Sinai is now
      in the sanctuary.

18 You ascended on high,
   leading a host of captives in your train
   and receiving gifts among men.
   Yes, even the rebellious live in your
   presence, O LORD my God.

19 Blessed be the Lord,
      who daily bears us up;
      God is our salvation.
20 Our God is a God of salvation,
      and to GOD, the Lord, belong
      deliverances from death.
21 But God will strike the heads of his
      enemies ...

19

EVEN THE REBELLIOUS LIVE IN YOUR PRESENCE

N o position is more seriously disappointing and more sadly disavowed in its outcome than the opinion that people can be divided into the unconverted, who rise up against God in rebellion, and the converted, who walk behind their Shepherd as obediently and submissively as sheep.

That was never the case! It's never been like that! And it never will be!

Just ask yourself who is more persistent in asking for the forgiveness of sins. Who does so from the depths of their soul and in spirit and truth? Who consistently feels deeply sorry? Who continually lies in dust and ashes before their God, brokenhearted and with psalms of penitence on their lips?

Do you think this is happening with the unconverted? Do you suppose it's the unconverted that resonate with an expression such as "How everyone laments, complaining about their sins?" If you do, you'd be sadly mistaken!

No, we do not question the fact that even the most defiant people now and then experience twinges of conscience and are unsettled. They have some impression of God's terrible anger. We know that even outside Golgotha's cross people can be shocked by their own wickedness. There can even be a tearful search for relief from sorrow without a tormented soul ever finding such a place.

The actual, steady, and increasing thirst for the forgiveness of sins you don't find with the children of the world. Nor do you find pleas for mercy there. Rather, these you find precisely with those that you would think rise far above the need for them. You find them only with the children of God. And you find them there not only at the time of their conversion or shortly afterward but until the day that they die.

They were rebellious. But because they are bound to the horns of the altar with cords of everlasting mercy despite themselves, they are always convinced in their heart of hearts that they are capable of fleeing that altar should their High Priest whom they confess ever cut those cords. But they are definitely no longer what they once were! On the contrary! They have become changed people! Earlier they would have found it horrible if they had thought that Jesus could capture their rebellious heart. But now, by way of contrast, they would find it horrible to think that Jesus would ever let go of their rebellious soul. Despite that being so, they remain rebellious people who are tied to Jesus with strength far stronger than their own.

To be sure, the stronger force with which they are bound to Jesus is no external force. It's not like the rope that a Levite used to force a bull or ram to lower its head before the altar. No, Jesus uses inner bonds. You can't see them. This is spiritual work. He binds you, and you don't understand how. He holds you securely, and you don't notice what he's using. Jesus even gets to the point of using that stronger force to keep your will in check, so far, in fact, that your will finally desires what at first it did not want.

But whatever is used to achieve that inner submission, the child of God here on earth retains the feeling until the day they die that something else keeps tugging at their soul. A power is working on it! The sense remains that if that power ever stopped working, they would snap loose like the stave of a barrel or like a rubber band released and that they would regress, far away from Jesus.

In actuality, things are going far better than that child perceives. But inwardly they feel deeper forces at work within that pull them away from Jesus. They want to follow along when Jesus leads with his tether. But even in that desire to go with him, a resistance is tugging and pulling in a different direction. It's as though the doorposts and window frames of a person's soul are sagging and crooked! The depths of their heart are exposed. And the pool bubbling up within is frightening. With brighter light, all the filthy splattering it produces can be seen. In the end, the self-conscious child of God sinks into deeper dejection that doesn't weaken but becomes stronger as time passes. They complain: "O Lord, how could my miserable heart be so terribly ungodly?"

That's what gives rise to the appeal "Cleanse me with hyssop!" And to the complaint "Lord, Lord, hear my prayer!" And when they hear from others who claim that they can no longer pray the fifth petition of the Lord's Prayer, they don't understand them. But they don't condemn them either; they simply say that they live by a different gospel than he does. They admit that they would be lying to God if they suggested otherwise.

Yes, God's children are rebellious until the day they die. But when they first recognize that Jesus is tugging at them, they know by that tugging that they are rebellious people who must live in God's presence. Living with

God! Above! In the Father's house! Willingly! In one of the many rooms that Jesus will have already prepared!

But for now they are still living in that hidden Zion, in the house of God that constitutes the church. In sweet communion! Enfolded in that secret fellowship of the redeemed! No longer living along with the world, but dwelling with God!

Yet, how?

In such a way that the Lord of the house could freely throw open all the doors, could dismiss the watchmen, and could loosen all ties to it! But look, if the Lord God did that, as terrible as it is to admit this, then all God's children who had not yet walked through the gates of death would scamper their way out of God's holy dwelling and fall into ruin. They know they would!

And just because they know that, and because they find it so horrifying should they lose touch with their God, they don't say: "O my Lord, I love you so much and am so confident of my situation that I know that you are capable of overlooking everything and that I will still dwell in your presence!" No, they say just the opposite: "O my God and Father continue to uphold me. Let your watchmen stay alert so that I do not slip away. Don't loosen the bands of your everlasting love, for things are good only in your presence. Only with you are things wonderful! Glorious! But my own heart would mislead me and my fleshly appetites would kill me. Like a sheep, I have so often wandered off and looked around instead of staying with you as your child. Show me your favor. In your grace, favor me by living in my heart."

The Savior hears that prayer!

And when he sees that we are rebellious and would like to flee from God but still want to live in fellowship with him, he comes with his reassuring comfort in the words of this unwavering promise:

> I have determined for the people's comfort
>> that even my conflicted children
>> will always live near to God.

Then he accomplishes it. He does what he promises. The outcome is that your rebellious soul is still living and keeps on living in the presence of your God.

¹² Behold, these are the wicked;
    always at ease, they increase in riches.
¹³ All in vain have I kept my heart clean
    and washed my hands in innocence.
¹⁴ For all the day long I have been stricken
    and rebuked every morning.

**¹⁵ If I had said, "I will say it like this,"
I would have been disloyal to the
generations of your children.**

¹⁶ But when I thought how to understand
    this,
    it seemed to me a wearisome task,
¹⁷ until I went into the sanctuary of God;
    then I discerned their end.
¹⁸ Truly you set them in slippery places;
    you make them fall to ruin.
¹⁹ How they are destroyed in a moment,
    swept away utterly by terrors!
²⁰ Like a dream when one awakes,
    O LORD, when you rouse yourself,
    you despise them as phantoms.

20

DISLOYAL TO THE GENERATIONS OF YOUR CHILDREN

Nothing makes as powerful an impression on a person who is isolated, abandoned, and living in loneliness as knowing that they belong to a people and generation for whom nothing can ever get any better.

If you only focused on yourself, you would simply give up. What kind of struggle is that when one weak person faces the whole world with all its smart, powerful, and influential people entirely on their own? They just laugh you off because of your beliefs, right? They just shrug their shoulders at your simplemindedness. Meanwhile, they fully enjoy the world. They are honored. They get ahead. And it's very obvious that they don't do with less because Immanuel is nowhere to be found in their lives.

But when you were first converted, that wasn't all so bad. Isn't it true that then you thought to yourself and a little voice inside you said: "Why do I need them? Let them have what the world has to offer. I have my God and his Christ, and I'm totally enjoying the love of Christ. Am I not even richer than they are?"

However, things didn't stay that way! While it's true that when your faith life was first kindled, its glow was indescribably beautiful. You were swept off your feet. It was like the warmth you felt from the hearth when, frozen stiff, you first came in from the cold. The inner sensation you had when first converted was even more glorious than that! That was the turning point. That's when you first drank from the Fountain of Everlasting Water. That was your coming through the Red Sea and seeing Pharaoh drowned; that was your celebration, deep in your heart, on the far shore.

But then you had to go through the desert. God's Word put it well for you: "The sufferings of the present time cannot be compared with the glory that will then be revealed." And the Lord's ambassador said it well when he exclaimed: "We walk by faith and not by sight." "In hope, we are blessed, and in nothing else!" But those positive words didn't register with you, and you thought that things would get better. Already now, in this life!

This happened because originally you did not understand the essence of faith. You still didn't grasp that believing is having nothing in your hands. And that was the complete opposite of what you were experiencing to be true. You hadn't yet seen that the certainty of God's blessing doesn't depend on what you experience, but on what God holds before you in his Word. Your response is not surprising. Faith is not something you learn from some little book. Not by going to a catechism class. Not in a sermon. Nor from what someone tells you. Only God teaches you what faith is when he causes you to believe and leads you spiritually into the faith. That's how he taught Abram to believe! And David! And Paul! He did it not by explaining it to them ahead of time, but by leading them into it. And that's how the Lord also does it now, today, with all his children.

It couldn't be otherwise. It had to be like this. That first overwhelmingly blessed experience had to eventually wear off in order to make room for fear, dimness of soul, empty-handedness, being at a loss for words, and branches without fruit. And that's when you first really got serious. The situation now became like this: those worldly folk really did have it good. They were at peace. They really did mock you. Now with respect to those people you in fact came to think that the world did have a lot to offer. But inside you felt so deprived, naked, and miserable that you would have been ashamed if they had been able to see inside you.

That's when faith actually broke through!

Having nothing, but still rejoicing! Rejoicing not based on your experience, but rejoicing because God's Word says you should! Believing based more on what God tells you to your face than on what your soul whispers to you. You got out of the way. God became everything—everything even in the inner working of your soul and in your becoming more holy. Believing, knowing, and being convinced that you were becoming holier in no other way than by, in, and from him. That was the change! He was accomplishing all this in you. He simply couldn't abandon this effort because it had been determined in his eternal counsel that all who are elect are chosen to become holy and blameless before him.

Whoever dares to acknowledge this comes to that point. Better said, they are there already!

But that happens only through fear, apprehension, and dying a thousand deaths. Then you will experience what Asaph did when his feet almost took him out the door, that is to say, when the thankless Asaph was ready to give up on his good and faithful God. He was at the point of allowing the most terrible curse to break loose in his soul. Then he thought it would be better to abandon God and to take up with the Evil One. But what restrained Asaph from such a curse at that moment? Or you can ask what likewise restrains every child of God dealing with a similar situation. God's grace does, you say, and you are correct! God accomplishes this. What I mean is this: How does that occur in the deliberating that such a troubled child of God does on those occasions? How do they work that out in the depths of their soul? Do they think about God? About Jesus? About his atoning blood? Oh, all of that only comes later! Their first response is completely different. It's totally understandable and completely human! They simply think that there's more of the same coming, that it's always been like this for the children of God.

If I were to say anything different, "I would be disloyal to the generations of your children!"

Whether he saddened his God didn't matter to Asaph very much at that moment. What did matter was that he was recognized as one who kept faith with his brothers. He thought: This huge crowd of witnesses has endured things like this for all these centuries. Now I'm one of them. I'm giving up and I'm going to find out what they loathed and identify with them in their drudgery.

Faithless? Not at all, for God has preserved me for this!

I'll never be a traitor!

That's when the loneliness disappears. That's when the spirits of all the completely justified surround us and when the martyrs wave their palm branches of victory over our heads. That's when we hear the angelic hosts rejoicing.

Praise God! I'm there!

The battle is over. Let the world enjoy itself and even mock me. And if in so doing they even scoff at God, I remain filled with holy confidence. I testify to them that I may definitely be despised, and naked, and have but few possessions, but in order to become a king ... by faith!

7 *Show us your steadfast love, O LORD,*
   and grant us your salvation.
8 *Let me hear what God the LORD will*
   speak,
      for he will speak peace to his people,
      to his saints;
      but let them not turn back to folly.

**9 Surely salvation is near to those who
fear him,
so that glory may dwell in our land.**

10 *Steadfast love and faithfulness meet;*
      righteousness and peace kiss each
      other.
11 *Faithfulness springs up from the*
   ground,
      and righteousness looks down from
      the sky.
12 *Yes, the LORD will give what is good,*
      and our land will yield its increase.
13 *Righteousness will go before him*
      and make his footsteps a way.

21

SO THAT GLORY MAY DWELL IN OUR LAND

Are the elect the only ones that matter? Aren't others affected as well? Is the ministry of God's Word intended only for the souls of some for eternity? Does the church on earth have no other calling than to awaken faith in those whom God calls through preaching? Shouldn't we be concerned about reaching the masses? Don't the state and society matter as well? Does it matter what becomes of Sodom and Gomorrah around us, just as long as the little creek that is the church stays pure and trickles along between its banks?

"No, not at all," exclaims the psalmist in response. "That's not the extent of things at all, not by a long way. That's part of the picture, to be sure, but it's not the heart of the matter. What it comes down to, and this is true for all generations, is that God receive his glory and that he be feared."

You may not push the elect to the foreground. The electing God is in the foreground, and he remains there eternally.

He is the glorious, almighty, and living God, the spring and fountain of all that's good. He's the overflowing source of all that lives, whether in nature or by grace.

Do you suppose that it's enough if only the elect benefit and if those that aren't do not? If so, you'd be standing in the way of God receiving the glory that is rightfully his. Then you'd be not the least bit worried about what goes on outside the circle of the Lord's people.

But if you regain the right perspective and see that the elect have a subordinate importance, you'll give more weight to everything around you. You'll also come to appreciate once more that God is above all and that the honor of his name is the only measure of all things. Self-centeredness falls away rather automatically.

If I'm a Father, the Lord says through Malachi, where is the honor due to me? And if I'm the Lord, where am I feared? What father is not affected by his children's scandalous conduct or when his good name is discredited by the terrible way they live? And how can Almighty God look on with indifference when a country here and a group of people over there cause enormous damage and behave like animals? They are the most exceptional of all his creatures, yet they debase precisely what's exceptional about themselves!

God lives. He reigns. Moment by moment he is also the Almighty God who has called into existence every tribe, city, village, household, and person. He not only created them, but he also sustains them and allows them to go on living by his powerful Word.

He alone is the God who is generous, gracious, and favorably disposed. He feeds and sustains every city and village. He makes corn grow in the fields. He protects people by his laws and comes to them through the preaching of his Word.

Would it really matter, then, to such a God how things are going, what's happening, or whether honor or scandal prevails as long as the people of the Lord are doing well?

No, I tell you, that's getting it backward. That amounts to saying God exists for the elect, when in fact his Word instructs us so clearly and firmly that both the elect and all his other creatures only exist for his sake.

Causing all other creatures to exist and upholding them in their existence, especially all peoples and nations, entire cities as well as hamlets and villages, serves a purpose. This is not only a future purpose but a present one. It's a purpose for today, for the time in which we are living. And what else could that purpose be than that the Lord God be glorified by all those cities and towns and villages?

If attention were focused only on the elect, you'd necessarily miss the life going on in the entire world. Then the entire world isn't needed for the preaching of the Word. Once impacted by it, the souls of those responding to it are never finished with him who is their Fountain of Salvation.

The world is still there with all its treasures, its rich flourishing of life, its natural beauty, and all its developments in human affairs. All of this is significant to the Lord. These are not simply toys with which the ungodly amuse themselves before having their last meal and leaving for hell. All of these are treasures given by God—the silver and gold as well as the rich flourishing of life in art and science. God created it all. It belongs to him. He is worthy of it. To regard all of this rich, full, shining reality apart from God is to hold a very impoverished view of who he is.

No, this is the same God who at one time paid special attention to Nineveh, that enormous city with many people and much livestock. The same God is still the owner because he formed all this. He possesses it because he upholds it. He rules it because he determines its destiny. He is this same God for every country and region, every people and nation, every city and village, every hamlet and neighborhood and settlement. Even in the remotest of places, no tenant farmer can be living in such isolation that this holy, glorious God does not claim his glory from that little patch of ground and the people living there.

Things need to be done properly. Light needs to shine in the darkness. Proper order and conditions need to govern human customs. Life's clockwork must run daily according to God's ordinances, and it must be properly rewound every evening through prayer and the confession of sins.

Passions erupt in every home. Sin churns in every village. Injustice erupts and rises to the top in every city. Ungodliness pulses through the veins of people's everyday living. But in these cases, here is where God's honor comes to expression. His name restrains those passions, reins in those sins, curtails injustice, and bridles ungodliness. It's to God's glory that the people in that house talk together again, that things are under control in that village, that justice is administered in that city, and that good laws are written for the country. This is a credit to him, strengthens his rights, and gives God victory over

Satan's terribly unholy power. It's to his honor most of all that where he extends his blessing day and night, he is thanked in city and countryside for his great compassion.

This is how every father needs to see things in his own home. He shouldn't only be asking how his children can be converted. Above all, he should be asking how his entire home can give glory to God.

As king in his home, he needs to say with David: "I will walk through my home with an upright heart. Whoever practices deceit will not remain in my house. The crooked heart I will keep far from me; the wicked I will not acknowledge."

This is how the mayor of every city and town must be an aggressive enemy of all injustice and root out all ungodliness. A private home is not his responsibility. In the home, the father is the mayor. But on the streets and with respect to all things public, the mayor must contend for God's honor. He must do so whether the law requires this or whether it does not. God Almighty will require from him the honor of his city or town. All drunkenness, dishonesty, lewdness, scandal, bitterness, and outbursts of hellish anger must be excluded from public life by him, or he will answer for it.

Likewise the king stands before God. What the father is called to do in his home and the mayor is called to do in his city or town, the king is required to do for the entire country and all the people. He is God's minister, the servant God has designated to see that God is honored in his country and that glory rises to the living God from the hearts of his people.

This is what the biblical Word teaches us.

This is what the Reformers clearly grasped.

This is what is still laid on the hearts of all Reformed people.

That's why we tolerate no yielding on this matter by our fatherland or its people.

If this were about us, we could. Because it is about God's honor, we cannot!

⁹ *All the nations you have made shall come*
   and worship before you, O Lord,
   and shall glorify your name.
¹⁰ *For you are great and do wondrous things;*
   you alone are God.
¹¹ *Teach me your way, O LORD,*
   that I may walk in your truth;

unify my heart in the fear of your name, O LORD my God,
¹² **and then I will praise you with my whole heart,**

   and I will glorify your name forever.
¹³ *For great is your steadfast love toward me;*
   you have delivered my soul from the depths of Sheol.
¹⁴ *O God, insolent men have risen up against me;*
   a band of ruthless men seeks my life,
   and they do not set you before them.

22

UNIFY MY HEART

Whoever prays, "O God, unify my heart!" recognizes that his heart is not unified but divided. He confesses to God, who fathoms the depths of our souls, that in a manner of speaking his heart is shattered into bits and pieces. He is no longer ashamed to admit that he is powerless to put them back together. He can't reunite them or weld them back into a coherent unit. Now, recognizing that he is unable to achieve this in his own strength, he approaches the Almighty, who has power over all things. He entreats God: "Please, Lord, work deep within me. Truly, O my God, unify my heart again; unify it so that I might fear your name."

Unity of heart. That's what this is about. That's what it comes down to.

Is there anyone who has achieved the incalculable strength needed to put such a smoothly operating heart to work? Wouldn't this require putting all the counsels and devotion of our souls into play? And even if that were possible, is there as much as one human heart that has the strength, capacity, and determination to work with the required purpose and intensity to achieve this? There isn't!

But that's the secret to understanding Satan!

Satan's heart is definitely unified. There is no division or disunity in him. There's not a trace of contradiction in the depths of his unfathomably evil heart. There's not a hint of any struggle in it. His heart is totally unified, and it's also thoroughly wicked. It's not only capable of hating God with his entire mind and all his strength; it's also filled with a passionate desire to do so.

That's also the secret that explains the influence that radically godless people have in church, state, and society today.

As long as we were dealing with a generation of people who were half-heartedly godless and only half-heartedly religious, the flood of godlessness was not overwhelming. It couldn't be while they were in control. They were too double-minded, too compromised, and too weak for that to happen. Their hearts were divided three or four ways.

But that's not the way things are now with the present pace-setting generation. Now a kind of person has appeared on the scene who has a unified heart. He wants to banish the fear of the Lord's name with all of his heart and with all of his soul. Just take a look at how things are going. Look at how people want to turn everything upside down and sweep away whatever gets in their way. A demonic, almost superhuman power has broken loose.

But yet, don't despair, my brothers and sisters. Simply pray that you will get what these evildoers have, namely, a unified, fused, and undivided heart. Do it because it's perfectly obvious that with a compromised and double-minded heart you won't be able to accomplish a single thing against those doing battle with you from the amazing strength of their own undivided hearts. As things now stand, half-hearted and divided efforts are completely useless, powerless, and ineffectual.

You can see how these swarming deviants daily gain more influence and how the half-hearted are simply sidelined. There's nothing at all to be gained by half-hearted piety, compromised orthodoxy, or half-baked theology. Now that the heat of the day has come, its light has burned off all these mists like shadows. The only thing that won't wither is what is deeply rooted in good ground. Only it can resist and remain standing.

This is how good comes from evil and God's people are aroused to jealousy by the unified hearts of godless folks. But this will happen only if they are provoked by the disgusting condition of half-heartedness and restored to wholeness. It will happen only if God Almighty hears their petition, "Unify my heart," and their hearts become one again. It will happen only if he hears that prayer and it convinces him that they "love him with all of their heart" and that they "wholeheartedly belong to him," the God of mercy.

Wouldn't that be worth celebrating?

So let's give thanks! Let's give thanks with lips that are resolutely serious about experiencing the beautiful days of renewed commitment once more. Evil has broken out, to be sure. But so has the richest, most glorious expression of heavenly power possible!

Let people focus only on this one thing. Let every individual first of all examine how things are in their own heart, in the heart they carry around in their own chest. Let them examine whether it is unified, whether it speaks with one voice, and whether it is whole.

And if it is not, then pray, pray without letup, pray at all times, pray to the Spirit who is within you and who prays with you, that the sacred peace of "a unified heart" may be given also to you.

I know very well that here on earth this is a petition that is never fully granted. But I also know that whatever is lacking in this respect is covered and fully completed through the unified, fully divine and fully human heart of the Mediator. It was never shattered. But through all the days of his life and all the times of his suffering, even unto death, it remained unified in the fear of his Father's name.

7 For we are brought to an end by your
    anger;
        by your wrath we are dismayed.
8 You have set our iniquities before you,
        our secret sins in the light of your
        presence.
9 For all our days pass away under your
    wrath;
        we bring our years to an end like a
        sigh.

10 **The days of our years are seventy**
    or eighty if we are strong.
    But they are filled with trouble
    and sorrow;
        they are soon gone, and we fly away.

11 Who considers the power of your anger,
        and your wrath according to the fear
        of you?
12 So teach us to number our days
        that we may get a heart of wisdom.
13 Return, O Lord! How long?
        Have pity on your servants!

23

TROUBLE AND SORROW

In our new, up-to-date mental institutions, people amuse themselves at the expense of the impaired in all kinds of ways. They do this particularly in the way they portray them comically. If possible, it should be pushed to the point that the impaired actually forget that they are mentally challenged. Yes, so far that it must seem to them that all their dreams, imagining, and fantasies accurately depict reality!

Well, we'll just leave that for what it is! As long as the church of Jesus Christ unlovingly thinks that it is completely free to leave dealing with the impaired in police hands, we will maintain our shameful silence about the atrocities that are part of life in mental institutions. When oh when will our diaconates wake up and promote a higher and nobler attitude about these things?

But where we won't leave matters is this: that our entire life here on earth betrays the same unholy attitude. It massages all our miseries. It characterizes our most intense pressure, tension, indifference, and insensitivity as a vacuous, make-believe display.

What the inebriated person does at their worst, we all do indirectly, step for step, and each in our own way. The drink that numbs the senses drags the inebriate out of the wretchedness of reality and magically transports them to a world of enjoyment and release. And what do the vast majority of people do besides close their eyes to the realities with which they live? They babble to each other about a life based on mere appearance, lies, and wishful thinking.

You could even take this to a deeper level. Suicide is the intoxicated person's escape at the ultimate level. A drinker sobers up eventually. The imaginary world they enter through their drinking soon disappears, and sober reality returns with double intensity. But, if there were some way to recapture that escape and to stay there forever, how could they do it? That's the way people get to the point of committing the shameful act and awful sin of suicide. The big difference is this, of course. The drink at least provides a momentary escape and release, while a person who commits suicide immediately stands in the presence of the terrifying God of whom the Scripture says, "Our God is a consuming fire!" Our souls recoil at this. Yet ... that which is sacrilegious and that which is terrifying increase in direct and sobering proportion to one another! So where oh where can we go?

How does this all happen?

Very simply, it comes from the fact that suicide and drunken stupor are nothing other than the most sharply defined manifestations of that same misguided desire for escape and for whatever promises more than it delivers. That's definitely a misguided desire, but it increasingly characterizes our entire lives, even among Christians.

God is exalted. He is long-suffering. His mercies are boundless. Merciful is even his name.

The Lord provides everything for us!

He knows eternity. He understands how endless the eternity of eternities is. And that's why he measures according to the full blessedness of his own divine being. That's the standard he uses for the indescribable and unspeakable glory that awaits the bride of Christ in his perfect heaven.

That's why God the All-Merciful makes every effort to draw us into his blessedness.

The Lord God finds it terrible that a person in the mere sixty or seventy years of their earthly existence would gamble away and discard eternity. In so doing, they lose the everlasting glory and the blessedness beyond description that will endure for a thousand times a thousand, and then times another thousand ages.

He, the Holy One, says: "My dear man, my dear woman, don't devote your existence to an empty life that is only so-so. But dedicate your entire existence to reaching my totally blessed and delightful eternity."

To be able to do that, rid yourself of all lies. Do away with false appearances. Represent things as they are. Challenge yourselves. Challenge others to face who and what they really are. You are miserable sinners. So are those around you. That's why misery clings to you all the days of your earthly existence. Your God is merciful. He is also the source of enjoyment in your life, and sometimes he even provides pure pleasure—that is, provided that you don't discount suffering and the serious side of life. For you wisdom is completely summarized in this one command: "Walk before my face. Pay attention to yourself in the same way that I, seated in my blessed heaven, see you as you really are. Recognize all the dark and unmentionable aspects of your life. Walk before my face with integrity!"

But people pay no attention to this. "You may not live that way," they exclaim! They wave a magic wand over their lives, as it were. It casts a deceptive glow about what is best and most beautiful for them. Life magically seems like heaven on earth. Enjoyment is everything. Life is about reveling in pleasure and staying excited without any memory of misery.

No time for prayer anymore. It's much too quiet at home. Get out into the streets! Go to the taverns! Take a walk in the park. Get tickets for the theater. Everything has to be seen in an aesthetic and light, even seductive clothing. Even hair on the head has to be stylized so that it no longer looks drab and ordinary.

And what about Christians? Oh, at first they struggle against these trends. They live separately. But do they go along with that deadened and deadening world? Sad to say, now they do. We know that there is a cross we must bear. But today we drape it with flowers, and it has become the cross covered with roses. Deep-seated seriousness has been wiped away by a love for light-heartedness. Even those who are presently preoccupied spiritually will soon succumb to the same thing. While for them this will be slightly different, essentially it will serve the same purpose. Keep quiet and stop preaching about the law. Don't talk about hell. I don't want to hear about my nakedness. Quit warning us about eternal damnation! People just don't want to hear any more about what they mock as "splashing around in mud puddles"! No, everything has to be about love, laughter, and enjoying luxuries. One person characterizes another as "a lovable guy," who in turn describes the first the same way. Pretty soon you have a whole circle of "really lovable fellows"! Naturally, in such a circle of angels on earth you find a lot of hearty laughing, even if it's about the real miseries and problems of life. Now we're dealing with something different stirring in the soul!

This is going to go on until the Lord intervenes.

He said in his Word: "The days of our years are seventy or eighty if we are strong. But they are filled with trouble and sorrow." And those of us who read this or even laugh about it succeed in making it come true. We do until we feel our own heavyheartedness and burst out: "God was certainly right about that. Trouble, trouble and sorrow, is the very best I've been able to find."

It's quite exceptional when God makes this happen.

Sometimes he allows people to go on living for years before they hear about a friend who passed away or about an acquaintance who had been unhappy and took their own life. But this person always simply thought: "Those are exceptions." Those reports were not enough to shake them out of their own fantasies.

They were told: "That's just how it is!" They had seen blow after blow fall on other people and simply thought:

"Sometimes it happens like that!" But they never applied those situations to themselves.

Then one day the Lord God finally knocked on their doors. Then they had to pick up the heavy crosses laid at their feet. Then they were brokenhearted. Then God put the terribly serious question to them: "Did I, your God, have it right, or did the world?"

Not that this is what happens to everyone. Not at all. On a battlefield where thousands lie wounded, no one amputates an arm or leg of those who are already gone. And at most they will spend only an hour helping those who are still alive but in serious shock.

There are also people, on the other hand, who live in a dreamland from the cradle to the grave. They enter life numb to its realities and die the same way. That's terrible. It's also terrible if God never visits them. It's terrible when he walks past our doors and doesn't amputate our maimed limbs. For then we are bastards!

There's something else that people don't quite understand, namely, that there has never been a single soul that God has not at some time struck on the outside before he has also totally broken them on the inside. As a rule, however, for us that is a blessed sign that God has begun an important work in us that will have eternal significance. At least that's true if he takes along his bag of instruments and begins his work of amputating an arm or leg.

How terribly, terribly hard our hearts begin pounding in fear when he does!

Sometimes a person cannot contain themself. They simply have to scream!

But God keeps on working. He does so with a steady hand. He works until the limb has been removed. He doesn't let up until his purpose has been achieved. He doesn't proceed by trial and error, and that's why he never makes a mistake. Once he puts his hand to it, he does a beautiful job. He also works through the fear of dying. Our God is the Great Physician. He heals.

This is what happens if the Holy Spirit is involved in this work.

There are also frightening operations that the Lord God performs simply to reveal his anger. God administers blows that only weaken people. They become hardened to them.

Who has not known such people? Look at Pharaoh and his circle. Consider the flood!

But let's leave this kind aside.

Suppose that the Holy Spirit mixes suffering with faith.

That bears fruit.

Here? On earth?

But I thought that all of that was reserved for what's above! Then what happens when the fruit is presented to God there, in eternity?

Look, that's when everything gets turned around. That's when we see things in retrospect and when we realize that for our entire lives we have really lived with an illusion. We saw value in things that had none.

That's when we'll realize that what we regarded as most important was filled with sorrow and trouble: our gold, our status, our influence, our physical health and strength, right down to our flesh-and-blood children and the "children" of our heart's desire. Everything on which we had pinned our hopes, we will then realize, gave us trouble externally and sorrow internally!

The only thing that will then be able to remove our trouble and quiet our sorrow is the Lord our God, whom we had forgotten so often and served so half-heartedly.

Then God, that God, will be most important of all!

The most important of all! That is exactly what he always wanted to be in our lives. But the root reality—the sinful root—has been that we have lived, sadly misled, in a spiritual fantasyland that could never be real!

PSALM 92

4 For you, O LORD, have made me glad by
your work;
   at the works of your hands I sing for joy.
5 How great are your works, O LORD!
   Your thoughts are very deep!
6 The stupid man cannot know;
   the fool cannot understand this:
7 that though the wicked sprout like grass
   and all evildoers flourish,
they are doomed to destruction forever;
8 but you, O LORD, are on high forever.
9 For behold, your enemies, O LORD,
   for behold, your enemies shall perish;
   all evildoers shall be scattered.

10 You will exalt my horn like that of a
unicorn:
I have been anointed with fresh oil.
11 My eyes have seen the downfall of my
enemies;
   my ears have heard the doom of my evil
   assailants.
12 The righteous flourish like the palm tree
   and grow like a cedar in Lebanon.

24

ANOINTED WITH NEW OIL

Why do we avoid the dominant image of work in our era? The human heart is very much like a workplace filled with an amazingly ingenious and complicated set of machinery. It throbs and pounds with the movement of every gear and coiled spring. The powerful, driving vitality of that inner workshop goes on day and night, busily occupied with our dreams and aspirations.

Our hearts can handle this. They are suited for it. Our nerves need to relax, but not our hearts. Think about this: the well-being of our souls depends on this state of affairs. At least, it does as long as all this activity goes according to God's plan and established order. It does as long as godly thinking controls our hearts. This driving force comes to us from above. It descends to us from Jesus himself. One part engages another so quietly and smoothly that our hearts don't even notice it. They don't even think about it. They only consider what needs doing for Jesus' glory and are sensitive to suffering for his name's sake.

But we lack the kind of harmony just described. Sad to say, the parts of our hearts no longer work together that smoothly and harmoniously. Satan wants to be the driving power at work in them rather than Jesus. Our gears move more at the direction of the world than that of Jesus. The result is that what was working smoothly becomes rough. What was polished becomes dull and speckled with rust spots. Our hearts cause us pain. The axle squeaks. The springs sag. The gears vibrate. We have the terrible impression that things aren't going very well for us at all. We sense that things aren't running the way God planned or wants. The result is that we weep. We cry tears of deep sadness in the hidden workshop of our souls. We yearn to walk in the ways of the Lord once again and according to his sacred plan.

If it comes to that, either in our prayers or without them, and always by sheer grace and never through any merit on our part, we are overwhelmed by the harmony that quietly and sacredly slips back into our hearts. It wipes away our bitterness. And in the depths of our hearts, we jubilantly cry out with the psalmist in his Sabbath rest: "Let God be praised. Strength has returned. I can function again. My horn is exalted like that of a unicorn; I have been anointed with fresh oil."

With fresh oil! It drips and flows between all the springs and gears in the soul's machinery. It makes smooth what was stiff and rapid what was sluggish.

It causes the whole inner apparatus to work with its intended power and purpose once more. Now we feel that something good is going on again. We are being productive. He who is the inner Source of power in our hearts causes his Spirit and strength to pulsate through the cylinders and valves of our hearts. The result is that something good is designed, shaped, and produced for his kingdom.

Or, if you want to use another image, suppose that there was no opening to the inner parts of your heart. Suppose there was no way for you to gain entrance to the treasure store of resurrection life. But suppose also that your merciful Lord opened that door and brought those treasures into every corner of your heart. As long as there had been no such entrance, you existed only in a state of broken fellowship. It was definitely not in the fellowship that God intended. He really needed to return. But it was broken as far as you were concerned, broken with respect to your soul's enjoyment, broken in preventing your life from flourishing. Heaven's windows were closed to you; the door of your heart was closed to heaven. Suppose that you repeatedly tried to force open its jammed bolts and to wrench open its locks, but nothing worked. They wouldn't budge. That's how stiff and stubborn they had become because of this world's damp, cold atmosphere. That's what prevailed until a good dose of "fresh oil" was applied to what had refused to budge, and until the locks finally allowed themselves to be opened. Then the door was open to God, and he entered your heart again. All the while he had been a faithful watchman. He had kept on knocking. He had called out persistently. Then, when you couldn't create an opening, God himself did, and he now refreshes you in his abundant love.

Or better yet, brothers and sisters, consider the imagery of Scripture itself. It doesn't think in terms of a machine or the stubborn bolts on a door. It points to man himself. Wearied by the heat of the eastern sun, he frets and is discouraged by the stench of his own skin. He coldly, impersonally regards himself as disgusting because of the odor it gives off, while the sharp sand stirred up around him stings his parched skin like sharp needles.

Give that man a bottle of fresh oil! Even if it's not a bottle of alabaster or nard, you would see immediately the eagerness and pleasure with which he pours it out and smears it into his foul, parched, stiff skin. That's because the miserable fellow is refreshed and revived by the wonder-working power of that oil. The terrible stench of his own skin that revolted even him is replaced by a pleasing, refreshing aroma that strengthens his spirits. Instead of brittle and cracked skin from head to toe, he has skin and muscle that is soft and supple and tender to the touch. The stimulating and reviving effect of that fresh oil penetrating the pores of his skin reaches his limbs and joints. It's as though its power touches bone and marrow. That's the power that this divine oil has.

So yes, that's how it actually, truly goes with those who have become spiritually stiff and brittle. That's how it goes for those whose stench of death rising from their own hearts had become a loathsome hindrance. That's how it goes when God, through his merciful Son, is again pleased to create something glorious and to the praise of his grace from the misery suffered by sinners. That's how it goes when in his most tender compassion he pours the fresh oil of his indescribable good will over our dried out hearts. That's what happens when Immanuel, God with us, once more becomes real in our inner experience.

Then things become possible again. Then we can do battle again in the struggle shared with the psalmist. It's the battle of becoming conquerors in him who is already victorious so that we might participate in his victory. Then the anointing with fresh oil is a renewal of our anointed purpose, our calling, and our sacred destiny.

Simply by knowing this, we receive strength for the battle again. The battle takes on a higher purpose whose outcome is guaranteed by our only Surety. What a blessing! It makes God's children celebrate, stammering: "You, O Lord, are everything; I am nothing!" Those are the sounds of a reconciled, redeemed, and revived heart!

5 *The mountains melt like wax before
the* Lord,
  before the Lord of all the earth.
6 *The heavens proclaim his righteousness,
  and all the peoples see his glory.*
7 *All worshipers of images are put to
shame,
  who make their boast in worthless idols;
  worship him, all you gods!*
8 *Zion hears and is glad,
  and the daughters of Judah rejoice,
  because of your judgments, O* Lord.
9 *For you, O* Lord, *are most high over all
the earth;
  you are exalted far above all gods.*
10 *O you who love the* Lord, *hate evil!
  He preserves the lives of his saints;
  he delivers them from the hand of
  the wicked.*

**11 Light is sown for the righteous
  and joy for the upright of heart.**

12 *Rejoice in the* Lord, *O you righteous,
  and give thanks to his holy name!*

25

LIGHT IS SOWN FOR THE RIGHTEOUS

Light is sown for the righteous! It is carried outside and buried in the ground. While for a time it is invisible, it is in fact germinating and swelling in the womb of the earth. Shortly the day of harvest dawns and overwhelms him with a wealth of light and brilliance.

Admit it! As an image this picture is choice and unbelievably beautiful.

The person who chose for God and in doing so broke with the world in his heart and with all that glitters here on earth sees that everything around him is gradually becoming darker. One light goes out in front of him, another behind him. Candelabras with their ungodly glow once burned wherever he partied, but now he has blown out their candles. Other little lights that could have kept on burning the world begrudged him. It blew them out just to torment him. Then there were also many other lights that the Angel of Light extinguished so that his soul might be purified. And now, step by step, he walks the path of his pilgrimage in almost total darkness. He becomes as exuberant as a child when now and then by God's mercy a lovely ray of light still falls across that path.

Pay close attention! We're not playing word games here or exaggerating. We can still talk about light, luster, and sparkle. The otherwise quiet joy and family happiness is still known to a fairly large extent by God's children. Who doesn't experience this and give praise and thanks to God for it? But what they lack and are compelled to do without is the worldly limelight, the glow of recognition, and the glitter of earthly glory. They aren't permitted to have it here on earth or it would cost them their faith and the soundness of their spiritual lives.

Yet such light is a big part of life today. We long for it. We've been promised that we can have it and not be limited to just a little subdued joy and sedate happiness. Our hearts are drawn to raucous shouts of laughter, the glamor of victory, and the glory of crowning recognition. But here on earth, we have to leave all that to those who are opposed to God. Those who kneel at the foot of the cross are not permitted to enjoy these things in their worldly, ungodly forms.

Daily experience makes this clear to you in repeatedly new ways. In our world here below, in the great drama of human life, slaves to their own egos bask in the light of recognition, just as Mammon in general and Satan do.

Meanwhile, God's saints and devout children are pushed into the drab background, where they are lost in a haze of darkness and obscurity.

The Holy Spirit knows all this. As the searcher of our human hearts, he also knows what this costs us, how this saddens us, and how this frequently threatens our faith. Remember, that's why he comes to us now as the Comforter and reassures us in this amazing song of suffering. He whispers in our souls: "The light of glory seems to have disappeared for you. But it isn't gone. It has simply been sown, that is, it is hidden in the womb of the earth so that when the world's day has run its course and your day has come, you will overflow in abundance—thirtyfold, sixtyfold, and a hundredfold."

So does the sower grieve when his barn is empty and his pouch drained because he carried his seed to the field and scattered it across the plowed ground? No, just the opposite! Now he finally feels completely satisfied. The seed is gone from the storehouse, and the field now shelters all of it beneath its cover. He knows that his seed grain is at work for him. He knows that God is causing it to flourish. He knows that by being hidden away, his precious seed promises to yield him a far richer harvest of wheat.

Should you be sad then, O my soul, because when Christ entered your life his angels followed him to carry out of your house the light of great honor and glory? That they dressed you in the clothing of obscurity? That people forgot about you and the world laughed at you? That the sons of Belial dragged you through the mud? That you were deprived of esteem in the eyes of men?

Understand that your light is a better light, a far more brilliant light. It definitely is and it always will be. It exists, although you may not see it during the long days and years given you. It doesn't shine far and wide, but it's hidden there, right at your feet, just in front of you, beneath the surface of your daily living. It's sheltered there for a purpose. It isn't inactive. But it's being protected by your God. There its luster is being steadily increased by his majesty, multiplied instead of diminished. It's gaining purity, clarity, power, and luster until it will eventually burst out. Then it will engulf you and wash over you like a flowing stream, O righteous person. It will flood over you and many others who are righteous along with you. It will make you shine with the splendor of your Lord, like a star in the firmament!

The psalmist sings that life for the ungodly is like a dense black thundercloud. Lightning flashes from it and lights up everything, but with a brilliance that consumes, destroys, and discredits (vv. 1–7).

But for you who follow in the footsteps of the Man of Sorrows where you live, love, and struggle, life may also be dark, to be sure. But that darkness is like that of the gray field holding the kernels of seed in its womb. They are sheltered there from the light while you ripen and swell until the time when everything that surrounds you is light, splendor, and glory (vv. 7–11). So "rejoice in the Lord, you righteous, and praise him in honoring his holiness!" (v. 12).

The one who said "I am the Light of the world" needs to be heard in terms of this light when he expresses the sobering prophecy: "If it is not sown into the ground and dies, it will always remain just one seed; but if it dies, it will produce fruit a hundredfold."

And he's that One whom we keep on following!

¹⁰ Some sat in darkness and in the shadow
of death,
    prisoners in affliction and in irons,
¹¹ for they had rebelled against the words
of God,
    and spurned the counsel of the
    Most High.

**¹² Wherefore he humbled their hearts
through hard labor;
they fell down, with none to help.**

¹³ Then they cried to the Lord in their
trouble,
    and he delivered them from their
    distress.
¹⁴ He brought them out of darkness and
the shadow of death,
    and burst their bonds apart.
¹⁵ Let them thank the Lord for his
steadfast love,
    for his wondrous works to the children
    of man!

26

THE HEART HUMBLED
BY HARD LABOR

Is it really above human nature to put someone down who thinks more highly of themself than they should and to keep them there?

And doesn't a Christian always struggle with thinking more highly of themself in their heart than they should? They know that they should be modest and humble and unpretentious because they live by grace, and that grace comes only to those who are lowly of heart. Still more, they have learned through experience that when they were proud, they became vulnerable to all kinds of bad things. Yes, they have learned that pride inflicts spiritual pain on their life and robs them of the sacred peace that God provides. But really now, what does that knowledge, or that conviction, or that experience really matter? Their arrogant heart won't obey them. It remains haughty no matter how much they beg and cajole it to be more modest once again. They have no control over it. Their heart controls them!

This is an extremely painful situation.

For a proud heart is not always expressed as craving greatness, fame, or honor in this world. Understand this clearly! It can just as often be an unholy desire not to be inconvenienced by anything, to not go out of their way for anyone else, and to always be headed in a selfish direction. It can be expressed ultimately in the most sinful pride of all, namely, in pitting one's own will against God's!

Don't be too quick to say: "That doesn't apply to me at all! Such thoughts never occur to me!"

Because, properly seen and measured, what else is every transgression of any of God's commands except elevating our hearts above the living God? He says: "This is the way it will be." But we protest, replying: "No, but this is how we'll do it!" In making that decision, we elevate our hearts above God. Ultimately, what the Lord commands, we oppose. It helps us as unholy mortals achieve what he forbids.

This is how transgressing God's commands always expresses an evil heart that exalts itself above God on high. This is the case with ungodly people as well as with those who have been born again. The only difference is that the ungodly do this without even thinking about it, but the born again are conflicted over it.

A child of God loses sleep over this. They are not at peace with it. They neither can nor will ever be satisfied with it. That's not because they are any better than the ungodly. Rather, considered in and by themselves, apart from Christ, they live in constant death. But the Holy Spirit is at work in the heart of a born-again child of God. A new person is emerging. And this new person "experiences a heartfelt joy in God through Christ. They possess a desire and love for living according to God's commandments." And so, when they feel like they're being attracted to sin and sucked into it, they sense an unaccountable oppressiveness slipping into them. This is being worked in the hidden recesses of their soul by the Holy Spirit, and it stirs them to want to circumcise the foreskin of their heart. They would rather die than upset and offend God any longer with their proud heart. They see with their own eyes what a contemptible creature they really are.

This is part of the suffering that God's children experience here on earth. This is the most painful and agonizing wound they feel.

Then they scrutinize everything, test everything, and evaluate everything in an attempt to rein in their proud heart. They pull back on those reins, manipulate them, and grip them so firmly that they think they have won the battle and can now sleep soundly. They think: "Things can't get out of hand now!" But sadly, all that effort only yields disappointment. The reins are ripped from their hands, and the first chance it gets, that proud heart suddenly swells again and rises up against God's commands. This happens even though they know and feel at that very moment that this must flout God, grieve their Mediator, and sadden the Holy Spirit.

But they can never afflict the Holy Spirit to such an extent that he does not return and comfort these "struggling children." They can never grieve this Mediator so much that he stops praying that they will return from their wandering ways. And they can never flout God but that he extends his hands and comes to their aid. And he does this by sending them "hard labor," since an arrogant heart is never humbled except by being burdened. Except by being pressured by the weight of divine anger! Then it is ultimately brought low and humbled by his strength and power.

At first the child of God doesn't realize this. Their first instinct is to push back against these afflictions when they come, to not want them, and to resist them in their heart. But that's only a momentary reaction. For then the gracious purpose God has in sending these burdens is made clear. This happens externally from the Word and internally by the Spirit. This heavy-handedness is not intended to shatter them but to help them in their continuous battle against their pride of heart. They realize that it isn't anger but mercy that is motivating God because he recognizes their frightful struggle to become humble without being very successful at it.

It's for this reason that he, your Father in heaven, the Always-Faithful One, and the All-Compassionate, has summoned these heavy burdens to descend on your heart. He desires the proud heart to bow down, to be brought low, so that in that humbled position the full stream of sacred, glorious, saving grace might appear and flow into your life again.

Then God's children rejoice!

They do so not because they realize that God is not vindictive. They do so not only because they are able to say: "This, too, has a saving purpose for me!" They do so much more because this is what they experience more profoundly and gloriously: "My proud heart has been genuinely humbled. Praise God! Grace has come!"

That's when they find themselves in the song of deliverance sung for them by the Holy Spirit in Psalm 107.

Because they had rebelled against God's commands and had rejected the counsel of the Most High in their unfaithfulness, he humbled their hearts through hard labor until they stumbled and realized that there was no one to help them.

But when they called on the Lord in their distress, he delivered them from their fears.

He guided them out of darkness and the shadow of death, and he broke their bonds.

Let them praise God for his tender mercies and for the wonders he has worked among the children of mankind.

168 I keep your precepts and testimonies,
    for all my ways are before you.
169 Let my cry come before you, O LORD;
    give me understanding according to
    your word!
170 Let my plea come before you;
    deliver me according to your word.
171 My lips will pour forth praise,
    for you teach me your statutes.
172 My tongue will sing of your word,
    for all your commandments are right.
173 Let your hand be ready to help me,
    for I have chosen your precepts.
174 I long for your salvation, O LORD,
    and your law is my delight.
175 Let my soul live and praise you,
    and let your rules help me.

176 I have gone astray like a lost sheep.
    Look for your servant,
    for I have not forgotten your
    commandments.

27

LIKE A LOST SHEEP

The lost sheep of Psalm 119 is not someone who is foolhardy and estranged from God. They are not a child of the world whose prayers are frivolous. They are not unconverted. But they are a child of God and servant of Jehovah. They are someone who keeps God's law and is penitent and converted. But they are the kind of person who, after believing, once again strays from the way of salvation. In the realities of daily living, that happens to such a "sheep" through mere negligence and lighthearted inattention.

By nature, a sheep doesn't act that way! It seems like the sheep of any given flock cling together so tightly that they can't live without each other. That's why they crowd together the way they do. It's as though they mimic God's cherubim living together. You can literally say about sheep and their flock: "Where one goes, they all go; where one stops and stands, they all stop and stand still as well."

A sheep is the most defenseless, helpless, and dependent animal imaginable. It is so constituted that it doesn't act, but it reacts like the others do. It doesn't lead, but it follows. It doesn't take initiative, isn't assertive, and isn't curious. This just isn't in its nature! Someone else has to find the pasture. Someone else has to lead them to a meadow and show them where to eat. Then a sheep eats. Then it lives. Then it is wondrously carefree.

But now consider what a separated sheep is like! The psalmist expresses it so graphically in a single word. A separated sheep is "lost." It's not only the case that such a wayward animal feels tremendously unsettled, but it looks for the other sheep of its flock. But they're not around. So it bleats for its shepherd. He doesn't answer. It longs for the meadow, but all around it are sand and rocks. What's even worse is that a separated sheep is totally helpless. Accustomed only to following, it hasn't a clue how to find the way back. It sees no path. It wouldn't know a path if it saw one. If it did, it would take it the wrong way. It just walks in circles there in the wilderness, without any idea where to go. Finally, it just collapses, tired of walking, totally fatigued, and lying against a rock, it begins bleating, and crying, and simply shrieking. What would it ever be able to do in such a situation if it weren't for the nipping of the shepherd's dog? The shepherd, the shepherd! He's the only one who can bring it back. Otherwise it would die. It would languish and expire.

Bless me with life, O my shepherd. Search for your separated, lost sheep!

So you can clearly see that by the lost sheep the psalmist is referring to a child of God and absolutely not to someone who is unconverted. What also strikes you is that he is talking about himself and not about someone else. "I, I myself am that lost sheep," he is in effect saying. "It is I who love God's law. It is I who find my satisfaction in keeping God's commandments. It is I who has been singing: 'Your loving care has never disappointed me.' But I have disdained your flock. I have lost sight of my shepherd. So now here I lie, gone astray and dead tired, humbled and lost. I'm left with only one defense against fighting off complete destruction. I can still simply cry out: 'Pour life back into my soul!' I can still confess: 'I have gone astray like a sheep that has unwittingly lost sight of its shepherd.' But, contending with the Devil, hell, and the reproach of my own heart, I still glory in the language of faith that professes: 'I am steadfast in wanting to hear your call once more!' "

The psalmist did not get to the point of acknowledging his shame all on his own. The Holy Spirit forced it out of him. This is first of all and naturally because he was the one who was searched for, found, and rescued. He was the one who was returned to the pasture of God's hidden joys, to the flock that God loves, and to the watchful eye of the Good Shepherd. But all of this occurred for a higher purpose.

The apostle says that all that was written earlier was written for your benefit. It was written so that you might find hope in the patience and reassurance expressed in Scripture. This is why the Holy Spirit compelled the psalmist to describe the state of his soul like that of a lost sheep. It's why he moved him to put it in song and to sing it. It wasn't only for the psalmist's benefit but for that of all God's estranged children. It was to shed light on the separated and lost condition that can overcome your heart. It was so you might discover yourself in these closing words of the psalmist's song. It was so you could grasp the clear, helpful, pure truth about yourself once all the empty, imaginary interpretation of these verses has been wiped away. It was so that you could be brought to the point of exclaiming: "Yes, that really lays out my situation with God truthfully. That's how it is with my soul! O God, be gracious to me, a poor sinner!"

This creates patience. This brings comfort from Scripture. And by way of patience and comfort comes hope. Hope, yes; but definitely not the hope that we will be able to stumble across some little stream or find a small patch of green pasture grass by ourselves. That's not hope at all. It's false hope. For if our souls react like that, it's as though the sand is more parched, the rocks are all the hotter, and everything around us is mocking our separated souls' sense of being self-sufficient.

Nor is it the hope that by trying once again, we will finally find the correct path back. That's because if we take to heart what the psalmist spoke from his heart, we are blind to that path. We can't see it anymore. We wouldn't recognize it if we could. And we wouldn't be able say whether it headed east or south.

No, that hope consists only and entirely in the fact that we're able to believe again. We're able to believe that we have the kind of gracious Shepherd who would leave his other ninety-nine sheep behind in the wilderness in order to start looking for the one that was lost. We're able to believe in a Shepherd who is incapable of thinking: "Well, that sheep is gone anyway. It's his own fault. Just let it stay lost!" Rather, he says to himself: "That one sheep is also one that I received from the Father!" So out of respect for his Father's will, he sets out and searches for that sheep until he finds it. He doesn't quit until he does.

That kind of hope comes because we believe again. It comes because we believe that we have such a mighty Shepherd that he has the ability to find the exact spot where we're lying down. He's so strong that no matter what the distance is between us, he's able to hear our souls moaning for him. Whether it's over cliffs or through treacherous terrain, nothing is too painful or too difficult for finding "the lost child" and returning them to their God and ours.

Let me ask who is so lost that they cannot be found?

Not someone who says: "Lord, I'm going to come looking for you!" But one who cries with all the energy left in their faith: "Lord, search for me, your servant!"

Not one who appeals: "Save me so that I may yet live!" But one who implores: "Favor me with life so that I may still praise you!" One who dares to testify, even when they lie near death: "I am steadfast in listening to our voice!"

Yes, truly, God comes quickly for such as these. He finds them again. They shall yet praise him!

If this is how things are with you, my brother and my sister, then lift your eyes to the mountains, from where your only help can possibly come. That's where he beckons. He beckons from afar. Your good and faithful and divine Shepherd beckons to you!

To see him again is to live again! Isn't that true?

The person that sees him again can praise him once more.

Therefore, praise him, all his people! For all his people have gone astray, but they have all come through that experience.

We were all lost sheep, each in our own time and in our own way.

PSALM 121

1 *I lift up my eyes to the hills.*
   From where does my help come?
2 *My help comes from the* LORD,
   who made heaven and earth.
3 *He will not let your foot be moved;*
   he who keeps you will not slumber.

4 Behold, the Keeper of Israel
   will neither slumber nor sleep.
5 The LORD **is your Keeper;**
   the LORD **is your shade on your right**
   hand.

6 *The sun shall not strike you by day,*
   nor the moon by night.
7 *The* LORD *will keep you from all evil;*
   he will keep your life.
8 *The* LORD *will keep*
   your going out and your coming in
   from this time forth and forevermore.

28

THE LORD IS YOUR KEEPER!

I sn't it in conflict to say on the one hand that "God only gives grace to the humble of heart" but to say on the other hand that "one to whom grace has been given knows that they have been elect from before the foundation of the world"? Or doesn't the sense of being elect make a person arrogant? If so, isn't this the direct opposite of being humble? And doesn't that render a person unsuited for receiving grace?

And turning things around, if my soul lives in a state of being genuinely humble, don't I find myself so far down in the dumps that it becomes impossible to believe that such a miserable person as I can be one of God's elect?

And here's the proof! Don't you consistently find callous, proud people without an ounce of humility who offend and repulse you when you consider that they might be elect ahead of you? And don't you often encounter genuinely spiritual, tenderhearted souls who exude the fragrance of the Holy Spirit and who, with their low self-esteem, hardly dare to hope that they are chosen? They wonder whether there is as much as a twig or sprout inscribed with their name among the living branches grafted onto the True Vine!

So tell me, can you ever avoid the impression that those who say they are elect are often far from it, and those who don't dare to think they are really belong there?

And how do you see yourself on this?

Or doesn't the tension of this contradiction burrow its way deep into your soul? Don't you experience the following struggle? On the one hand, you sometimes believe that you are elect, it's true, but then you immediately feel trapped by your pride. But on the other hand, you subsequently become dispirited and stand before God in fear and trembling that you dare hope to share the joy of God's children.

Is this normal? Does being bounced between the poles of pride and fright have to endure to the end? Or according to God's Word, might not the Holy Spirit seem powerful enough to work both effects in you simultaneously? Isn't he capable of keeping you humble before God and at the same time joyful in the complete certainty that you are one of his beloved children?

Should you ask where the key to reconciling that apparent contradiction might be found, just read what the Holy Spirit says in Psalm 121 about keeping your heart. For what do we find there?

Just this: it says that "the Lord is your Keeper"—definitely that! But it also says that he is your Keeper because he is "the Keeper of Israel, of his church, of his Son's body"—and right here is the key to the secret.

Think about a pocket watch, one for example that you carry with you wherever you go. It contains any number of rotating little wheels and spindles, tiny screws and springs, minute nuts and shafts. And you protect that entire device encased in gold or silver with the greatest possible care, so that not even a speck of dust gets into it. You protect the entire thing, and in its entirety every small, insignificant, and trivial stem and screw that's part of it. You do this not because that little steel shaft is so valuable in and of itself but because it's part of the whole.

Removed from the watch, such a little pin would not be worth a tenth of a cent as a piece of steel. Thus it has very infinitesimal economic value. And yet you encase that infinitesimal little pin in silver or gold and attend to it with the greatest of care. You do so not simply for the sake of that small stem but because the entire intricate device that constitutes that watch simply cannot do without it. Taken by itself, it is scarcely worth the trouble of even throwing away. But as a part of the whole, it is just as essential as the little wheel spinning on it. In fact, so much of the entire device depends on that small shaft that the manufacturer has selected it with the greatest care. He did so not because of the value it has in and of itself. But by choosing it and inserting it into the entire device, he made it valuable.

This is exactly how things are between you and the God of Israel.

The Israel of God, the church of Christ, the body of the Son, is an intricate and well-crafted watch, if I may put it like that. Divine mercy is transmitted through its rhythmic functioning and daily ticking. In that watch there are likewise a countless number of little parts. We call them believers. Brought together in the whole body, they have their place like the rotating little wheels and springs, the spindles and tiny shafts, of a watch.

You, too, when considered in isolation and by yourself in that marvelous device called the church of God, are a completely worthless little shaft, maybe the most infinitesimal and insignificant one of all. You couldn't think of yourself as small and insignificant enough, therefore. Literally, hardly worth throwing away, like a tiny shaft or screw in the watch! But when God incorporates you into that device, and when he devises a place for you somewhere in that watch so that you are clothed with a purpose in it, the picture changes completely.

The Lord God has made and shaped and elected you for a place in it with unending skill and care. He's done so with even more skill than the watch maker in Geneva chose his little nuts and spindles. The holy God of Israel bestows, confers, and assigns a value on you that does not inhere in your own insignificance. Not for a moment! But it is yours only when you fulfill the service assigned to you in that role of a lowly little part in that beautifully crafted whole.

Then God protects you. He does this not because you are so insignificant. He does so because you are part of the whole, an intricate part of the entire and beautifully crafted timepiece. This is the church, the Israel that is the product of his desire. And now he encases you in silver and gold. He shields you from damage. He even sees to it that no speck of dust finds its way in. This is when the Lord is your Keeper, but only because he is the Keeper of Israel.

So now can your own soul tell to me whether there is really any so-called conflict between being "lowly of heart" and yet "chosen of God"?

PSALM 130

1 *Out of the depths I cry to you, O LORD!*
2 *   O Lord, hear my voice!*
Let your ears be attentive
*   to the voice of my pleas for mercy!*
3 *If you, O LORD, should mark iniquities,*
O Lord, who could stand?

4 **With you is forgiveness,**
therefore you are feared.

5 *I wait for the LORD, my soul waits,*
*   and in his word I hope;*
6 *my soul waits for the Lord*
*   more than watchmen for the morning,*
*   more than watchmen for the morning.*
7 *O Israel, hope in the LORD!*
*   For with the LORD there is steadfast*
*   love,*
*   and with him is plentiful redemption.*
8 *And he will redeem Israel*
*   from all his iniquities.*

29

FORGIVENESS AND
THE FEAR OF THE LORD

The twelve articles of the Apostles' Creed don't only include "I believe in God the Father, the Almighty"; or, "I believe in Jesus Christ, his only begotten Son"; or, "I believe in the Holy Spirit." They also include that more puzzling and more incomprehensible "I believe in the forgiveness of sins." Does this affirmation really speak truthfully to your heart so that you can add a hearty "Amen" to it?

To believe that an actual, living being called God exists; to believe that that God has revealed himself in the flesh; and to believe that this God really lives in people's hearts— all of this is already so indescribably immense and so unspeakably glorious that no human heart could have ever actually come up with these ideas by itself!

But if you once get to the point of confessing these things because God gave you the gift of faith, can you go further? Can you add the confession that this invisible God, this thrice-holy Being, forgives all your misdeeds? That he does not hold you accountable for your sins? That he has covered all your transgressions? Admit it, my sisters and brothers, doesn't this require a uniquely special grace? Doesn't it rise astonishingly far above anything that can possibly come from the depths of the human heart?

"I believe in the forgiveness of sins!" To say that and to mean it, and to really cling to it as completely true is something else. To do so when you have been shattered by wrestling with the depths of your sin is to understand something quite amazing! Or to do so when you have felt Satan's traps snap shut on your soul! Or when you have discovered how your enemies the Devil, the world, and your own flesh are capable of attacking you from three sides all at the same time! Or when you have experienced the indescribable anger of the Trinity against you as a stage in your salvation! Or when in the frightful oppressiveness in your soul you come to know that in the final analysis your sin is the most terrible sin possible! Or when the prayer "O God, be merciful to me, a poor sinner" is transformed from a prayer for conversion to the despairing cry of one already converted! So now you tell me, in the light of all this, when your soul has been shaken in its depths and you have been deeply shocked by your own shameful sin, whether even then you can calmly, with complete certainty, and in a spirit of quiet thanksgiving confess: "I believe in the forgiveness also of my own sins." Isn't doing so a much deeper mystery than confessing to believe in the three persons of the Trinity?

Oh, I know that people play games with the forgiveness of sins. They play with that tender reality like we play with other holy things of the Lord. We sing thoughtlessly. We pray when our heart isn't in it. And we all also talk about the forgiveness of sins without any feeling. (Lord, how is any of this possible?) It is considered unimportant, even less than unimportant, that people admit that they don't have a clue how the sacred Lamb of God could possibly be a substitute for us.

Worse yet is that we have not only played games with the forgiveness of sins, but that each of us has sinned in this connection in our own way. "God is so good and God is so loving. Even to ask for forgiveness is really unnecessary. God forgives automatically. How could he stay angry, this loving Father in heaven?" That's not only the way modernists talk. It's also the way the modern sinner living in our own heart speaks, or better said, the old sinner in our own heart. Just think about this for a minute. Satan knows how to manipulate everything. He even sees an opportunity in the forgiveness of sins to cause new sins to grow in our evil hearts. Listen up; it's all really very simple. He does nothing more than push aside preoccupation with sin itself and replace it with a focus on the forgiveness of sin. When he does that at the point where we are about to sin, our minds focus on the grace of God. We say to ourselves as we are about to fall into sin that we will be forgiven immediately! That's when the last connection we have with God's covenant of grace is cut. And we fall. We fall deeply. We do what God sees as sin. Oh, the unfathomable mystery of evil! Then our impure lips pray the prayer asking God to forgive us even for that sin.

Children of the kingdom, you have to realize this. Nathan's word applies here. It applies to your soul and not to someone else's: "You are the man!" But that point has not yet sunk in. The promptings of your own heart don't get it! Seen another way and equally true, there is a type of faith in the forgiveness of sins that is not from God but from the Evil One. This is a faith that dares to say, "With you, O God, is forgiveness, therefore all fear of your holiness is gone from left my heart."

But that is not the confession of the church of Jesus Christ.

What sets the tone of her life is exactly the opposite. It is expressed in the ancient song of ascent: "With you is forgiveness, therefore you are feared!"

"Feared" not with a fear that causes us to flee from God! But fear as a holy emotion and a profound awe that, approaching God in his exalted majesty, causes us to stop in our tracks with reverential silence. It purges us of unholy thought. It compels us to uncover our heads, to open our ears, and to listen respectfully to what the Lord says.

And what he says is this: "My child, don't commit that sin any longer." When God's child hears their Father say that, they find that they cannot, even when in their wickedness they are still inclined to do so. For then the voice of God is like a restraint operating in their souls and holding them back. This is the God who has forgiven all my sins. This is the God who caused the precious blood of his dear Son to flow. And this is the God that continuously appeals to my heart, "My child, don't commit that sin!" That's when the untrustworthy and afflicted soul shows fear, and that's when it neither wants nor dares to go against the voice of God. For he who calls out to them like this in his soul-piercing voice is the same God who has forgiven all their sins.

This is how evil is disarmed. This is how sin is stifled at birth. This is when a sneering Satan retreats. In this God is praised.

And this is how the fear of the Lord comes through being forgiven.

At this point the church of all ages exclaims, "Yes! Amen! With you is forgiveness, therefore God is feared!"

So tell me, with what choir are you singing?

Where, when your soul dares to confess, "I believe in the forgiveness of sins!"?

Does it sing that song superficially and without feeling to the tune of the thoughtless? "Forgiven … so, not really so concerned about sin!"

Or for you has it become an overwhelming power of God in your chest? "I am no longer able to commit sin, because God forgives!"

Reader, be discerning in answering that question. For once don't trust your own notions, or your personal feelings, or your own understanding with respect to this confession. But examine the actual way your own soul works.

Does your faith that God forgives sins render your conscience more sensitive or more indifferent?

How terrible if you have to admit "more indifferent."

But, then, it is better that you are startled now than that you enter eternity with a devilishly misled faith in your heart, only to stand quivering and shaking before God when you do.

That particular sin, the sin of your misled and unrealistic and false believing, is especially abominable. It is an abomination in the presence of our Holy God.

But there is still hope.

That's because there is even a way back to the thrice-holy God for the soul that is suffocating with that particular sin. It is to come with the language of the psalmist on one's lips:

"Lord, with you is forgiveness, forgiveness even for this sin, therefore you are feared!"

PSALM 131

1 O LORD, my heart is not lifted up;
   my eyes are not raised too high;
I do not occupy myself with things
   too great and too marvelous for me.
2 But I have calmed and quieted my soul,

**quiet like a weaned child with its
mother;**

   like a weaned child is my soul within
   me.
3 O Israel, hope in the LORD
   from this time forth and forevermore.

3 0

LIKE A WEANED CHILD

A child nursing at its mother's breast is still living in the initial luxury of its young life. But even in that luxury it's still unsettled. It always wants the breast again because the breast never fails to provide in abundance. That child feels intensely how much it cherishes the breast, especially when its thirst for its mother's milk returns.

But now consider the same child after it has gone through the process of being weaned. I'm not thinking about it during the process of being weaned, but after it has been weaned. The time of always crying to be fed has passed. That little child has learned to take a more measured approach to eating. If you set it on its mother's lap now, it's no longer drawn to her breast, but it sits there blissfully, simply basking in its mother's presence!

And isn't this the way it is for the soul in its transition from the turbulent conversion experience to the sense of peace that follows? Isn't this similar to the experience of a weaned child? Isn't the recent convert like a nursing child in always dreaming about the bounty of divine love? By drinking deeply, isn't it refreshed by its new source of life? Doesn't it take in more than weak, infant faith can possibly swallow? And in its restless and intense prayer life, isn't it always asking for an even fuller stream of divine grace?

But then the soul that was initially satiated by such bounty goes through a disillusioning experience. It is weaned from being overly excited, from the excess it enjoyed, and from what is too wonderful for this world. It still focuses on divine love, but it is now a love tempered by Golgotha and the sobering reality of the cross. It now takes the measure of things more dispassionately. A spirit of longer-term expectation replaces one of urgent immediacy. Now it imbibes a sense of what the soul needs to endure. Former unsettledness is replaced by a growing sense of peace. This is like the peace of a child that first drank milk but that has now been weaned from it and asks for its mother as mother. The maturing believer now looks to God as God, and prays with humble entreaty, knowing how very small one's soul really is.

What we have here is an example of deep dependence. An even greater dependence than that of the little child nursing at the breast is that of one who has been weaned. The little child on the breast is willful.

That breast belongs to it! That breast is there for it! The mother's warm breast is its little kingdom! With its own tongue and little lips it sucks the lukewarm milk! It's very different for the weaned child. That child has nothing. It discovers that nothing has been prepared. It eats right along with what others eat. And it even lacks the ability to bring to its mouth by itself the food that has been set before it. Its dependence is total!

And is this also how it is for you who have been weaned from the bounty of your first love? Don't you now feel small and dependent in your heart? You first thought so much was possible! You were so satisfied in your own little kingdom! You were always ready to express yourself on everything. Your lips were always ready to sing God's praises!

But if you're honest with yourself, haven't you now developed appreciation for what's small? Don't you take pleasure in the lowly state of God's servants? In the fact that you encounter opposition? That you're denied honor and status? That your plans and aspirations fail, so that you now come to enjoy with a joyful heart all with which God has favored you? With a measure of resignation, haven't you learned to testify with David: "O Lord, my heart is not proud. I will not concern myself with things that are too great and wonderful for me. I'm like a weaned child with its mother, and my soul is like a weaned child within me. Israel, hope in the Lord!"

Let me say this yet. A mother's milk is also bread, as Augustine so beautifully put it. But it's bread that has passed through a mother's veins and become milk. Bread, therefore, but by derivation. Bread, therefore, but bread first enjoyed by someone else so that the suckling could also enjoy it. Sweetened, weakened, and broken down!

But as soon as the small child is weaned, it gets solid food and it eats actual bread. This is bread that is softened and broken into small pieces. But it is nevertheless bread, bread with all its nourishing elements that make a person strong.

And now isn't that just the way it happened with you when you were brought to your Savior, who is your Bread of Life? Initially you had more desire for that Bread when it had passed through another person and become for you like "mother's milk for a newborn child." People fed you from Christ, but Christ himself still remained distant to you. The Word was still too difficult for you, too demanding, and too indigestible. Then you had no desire for the Word other than as blended with a sweet little song and as reworked into a very light meal with all the seeds and pits and removed.

But now that you've been weaned from the bounty of your first love and have developed a desire for what's much more modest, you have an appetite for the Bread of Life himself. That's because you are no longer a "new-born child in Christ." Now the hard crust that covers the Word that inside is soft and chewable no longer deters you. Now you patiently bring to your lips the bread of the Word that has such a heavenly, life-giving aroma. And what's now missing is the mammoth pretense of thinking that you already know everything. All your knowledge in fact fails you! You really know nothing! And crying out from your blindness of soul, you wait for the light from your Only True Love. And in that waiting you sit like a weaned child with its mother, quietly content in the presence of your Lord!

³ *On the day I called, you answered me;*
   my strength of soul you increased.
⁴ *All the kings of the earth shall give you*
   thanks, O LORD,
      for they have heard the words of your
      mouth,
⁵ *and they shall sing of the ways of*
   the LORD,
      for great is the glory of the LORD.
⁶ *For though the LORD is high, he regards*
   the lowly,
      but the haughty he knows from afar.
⁷ *Though I walk in the midst of trouble,*
   you preserve my life;
you stretch out your hand against the
   wrath of my enemies,
      and your right hand delivers me.

⁸ **The LORD will complete what he began**
   with me.
Your mercy, O LORD, is everlasting.
Do not neglect the work of your hands.

31

DO NOT NEGLECT THE
WORK OF YOUR HANDS

Nothing weighs on hearts or crushes and haunts us more than our weakness with respect to the work of our hands.

A farmer experiences this when he plows and harrows, sows and weeds, but then can do nothing at all about the growth. In order to reap a good harvest, he is deeply dependent on the rain that falls and the sun that shines on his field.

It requires faith and courage to plant a stand of oak trees. That's because you understand when you place acorns in the soil that they germinate very slowly and grow even more slowly! You don't even think that you yourself will ever enjoy a harvest from what you've planted.

The construction of huge cathedrals like those of Cologne or Strasbourg that went on for centuries wasn't undertaken by a generation so egocentric that in considering the success of their immediate task they thought their work was finished.

That same sense is of extended time is felt even more strongly by everyone who devotes themselves to the moral work of building the invisible temple of the Lord.

Simply consider the basic scope of rearing your children. How often don't you face this with a sense of powerlessness and embarrassment? Someone else puts much less of their best effort into this than you do. They hardly ever complain about it. They virtually permit their children to grow up wild, but amazingly they turn out well. But your children, on the other hand, for whom you pray every morning and every evening, seem so much less loving and appear to have almost no fear of the Lord whatsoever. They weigh heavily on your heart. You cherish them as the apple of your eye. You nurture them in the fear of the Lord with the greatest care. Despite this, they arouse your growing concern. But you persist and certainly never even think of letting go of them! You don't know why you react this way, but you don't ask about it. You can't do anything else. Nor do you want to! In fact, you must not. That quiet nurturing of your offspring is automatic and unconstrained.

Or have a look at our Christian schools. Isn't it discouraging when you sometimes see that a generation being nurtured in a secular school begins to inquire about God once again, while the results in our own schools can be so contrary? Yet, isn't it the case that even then you don't stop giving sacrificially for the school building? And you continue to testify, despite negative results, that it's only a school based on the Bible that's strong enough to protect our people.

And it's true that this is exactly how it goes with all spiritual effort in the kingdom of God. In one congregation after another, an invasion of unbelief and modernistic preaching has swept away the old mustiness. It has also created spiritual ferment and a remarkable return to a lively faith. Meanwhile, elsewhere congregations blessed with the steady preaching of the Word unfortunately simply sleep through it and grow deaf to it. Nevertheless, you don't hesitate for a moment to continue to preach the Word or battle unbelief.

Take whatever field of endeavor you like. It could be Sunday schools, young people's groups, or missions to people of other faiths, to Jews, or to merely nominal Christians. It could be attempts to restore the state's involvement with the church or struggles to have the country's government submit to the power of the Lord. But you'd always give up in discouragement if you relied only on yourself. You would as well if you only considered your weakness, continual disappointment, and meager results. But that's not what you do. You keep on working. Rather than complain about your own sluggishness, you always work with renewed courage, stronger energy, and holier zeal!

This even happens, doesn't it, when in the depths of your soul you're engaged in a restless struggle to find greater peace, inner fellowship with the Lord, and more evidence of the power of the Spirit? It happens when these are even further diminished and you raise the sad complaint that you lack spirituality but feel spiritual depression and emptiness. In times like those, you never think about the state of your soul so that you abandon inner struggle or concede the battle to Satan. Rather, in some mysterious way that you can't explain, you then experience a higher, holier, and more exalted condition in your heart—definitely not with respect to your always-accusing awareness, but definitely with respect to your standing with God.

So how do you explain such an unusual experience in the context of human effort?

How do you explain always swimming against the stream like this and still prevailing? Facing so much discouragement but always maintaining courage? Confronting what's against all odds but never giving up and continuing to plant acorns when you will never see the greening of the treetops?

My good reader, you only explain it in terms of faith!

It's faith that everything is exactly the opposite from what it seems to be! It's faith that it's not really the person doing the work but that the real Worker involved is the Lord God. It's faith that they are a much smaller and less significant instrument in the almighty hand of God at work than the chisel is in the hand of a sculptor.

This is the faith that all of our working and striving and effort is of no use and produces nothing unless it is guided by inspiration from above. It reflects holy intuition. It proceeds blindfolded, yet it is guided unnoticed by our God with invisible ties to his eternal wisdom and tender love.

Realize this! Only a person who has this disposition of soul quietly continues working without asking about the outcome. Such a person realizes: "The real worker is actually the Lord my God. It's not I who is raising my children, but God is doing it. It's not I who is doing the teaching at school, but the Lord is the educator. It's not I preaching, but the Lord himself causes his Word to go forth. It's not I who harbor tender desires for my people, but the Lord is the one keeping watch over them."

Then, if people are aware of this, the work is genuine. For God endures forever, and even if we sink away and disappear, his work always goes on. Then it doesn't really matter whether or not I see the results with my children if the Lord attends to them after I die. Then my work of bringing up my children is not in vain as long as it pleases God to cause the seed that I have sown to ripen in the next generation.

With that kind of faith, no effort is ever in vain. Then every endeavor comes to fruition quietly and peacefully. In that context, people pay attention to years rather than to days and to centuries rather than to years. Then at heart they consider people and conditions and momentary opportunities in terms of principles. Or, if you prefer, they see them in terms of him who is the Source of all things and who has the power to bring all things to completion.

A generation that lacks this kind of faith and this sense of eternity lives fast. Its work is driven at a feverish pitch. In just a few years, it magically causes half a city to appear on what was only bare ground. But you can push its houses over with your bare hands. On the other hand, the generation in which the work of God is going on is involved in building monuments that endure for ages. They reflect the praise and fame of their Chief Builder dwelling in the heavens, not that of the workers here on earth.

A sinner living without this kind of glorious faith struts around on the peak of their roof and in their pride exclaims: "Is this not the proud Babylon that I have built?" But for the sinner who is permitted to stand in blessed faith and does not ask about the outcome but keeps on working quietly in the service of their God, it is otherwise. They labor on behalf of their home, their country, and industriously for their school and the church of Christ. They always find strength and comfort in praying the prayer that was on the lips of David: "Lord, not my work, but your work be done. Complete the work of your hands."

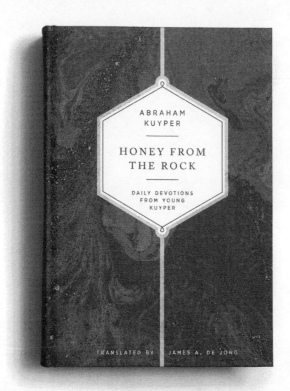